Management in a New Key
Communication in the Modern Organization

Second Edition

Management in a New Key
Communication in the Modern Organization

Second Edition

Alan Jay Zaremba, Ph.D.

Industrial Engineering and Management Press
Institute of Industrial Engineers
Norcross, Georgia

Quantity discounts available.

Institute of Industrial Engineers
25 Technology Park
Norcross, Georgia 30092

Originally published in 1989. Second edition published in 1993.
Printed in the United States of America
94   93   5   4   3   2

Articles appearing in Appendix C were originally published in *The Quality Observer* as part of a series titled "Communication and Quality." Reprinted with permission from *The Quality Observer*.

Library of Congress Cataloging-in-Publication Data:

Zaremba, Alan Jay.
   Management in a new key : communication in the modern organization
   / Alan Zaremba. -- 2nd ed.
       p.   cm.
   Includes bibliographical references and index.
   ISBN 0-89806-135-0 (pbk.)
   1. Communication in engineering. 2. Engineering--Management.
I. Title.
TA158.5.Z37   1993   93-21889
658.4'5--dc20   CIP

To

Dr. Robert Howard Zaremba

and

Matthew Adam Zaremba

Contents

Preface

The second edition of *Management in a New Key*, like the original, is based on the incontrovertible fact that management and managers cannot be effective unless there is an understanding of the inherent interdependence of communication and managerial activity.

People who are skilled, responsible, knowledgeable, or even unusually intelligent often fail miserably as managers because they fail to see the implicit relationship of internal organizational communication and managerial success. Those managers who do not acknowledge the importance of internal communication to their work will be unable to overcome the obstacles insidiously created by poor interpersonal and organizational interaction.

The objective of *Management in a New Key* is to explain the relationships of management and communication in a clear and digestible way. The book has been written for managers and those who aspire to be managers or business communication professionals. The intent is to provide an easy-to-read description of a subject that is crucial for management success.

The book has been organized so that it can be read in one of two ways. I suggest that readers go through the book sequentially, but for those who would prefer to, the book can be read section by section for a particular reader's need or interest. It is important to note, however, that an understanding of managerial communication requires more than just knowing how to make a presentation or how to run a meeting. The impact of communication on management transcends specific communication contexts.

This second edition also includes four appendices that may be of value to readers:

- Appendix A is an annotated bibliography of other books related to managerial communication.

- Appendix B is an annotated compilation of organizations and journals germane to managerial communication that might be of value to managers and those interested in researching this subject in greater detail.

- Appendix C contains three additional articles I've written on subjects specific to managerial communication. In each instance the article, to my way of thinking, is valuable for those who are truly concerned with communication issues in organizations. The articles relate to superior-subordinate interaction and sensitivity, technology and communication, and receiver orientation, respectively.

- Appendix D includes three cases that I suggest readers examine and attempt to solve. These cases may be valuable for group analysis in those organizations that are trying to improve their own organizational efficiency.

Further, an index has been added to this second edition, and there have been several internal additions and structural changes made to improve the readability of the book.

I want to thank Sonja Lee who did an outstanding job editing the second edition of this book. Also Carey Gifford, the manager of Industrial Engineering and Management Press, was helpful in the creation of this project. In addition, thanks to Kelly Jones who helped with the indexing and Monique Gagnon who also assisted with indexing and proofreading sections of the revision.

Among others who read the first edition and commented with suggestions, I thank New York State Psychological Association Executive Secretary Diane Kermani; Jack Turan, executive vice president of Briarcliffe College; Francis Battisti of Broome Community College in Binghamton; Brenda Gumbs of the Eastman Kodak Company; Dr. Andrew Rancer from the University of Akron; and my Northeastern colleagues Dr. Anne Mattina, Jay Halfond, Nancy Korn, Michael Woodnick, Linda Loehr, and President John Curry. In addition, thanks to Dr. Jerome Supple, president of Southwest Texas State University; Dean Kenneth Turow of the Culinary Institute of America; Dr. Binford Peeples of Memphis State University; Ruth-Ellen Greenwood of Humber College; William Walsh of William Walsh Associates in New York City; and Dr. Donald Rogers of Rollins College in Winter Park,

Florida. Also, I thank students who have read the book and provided constructive comments, especially Elizabeth Robinson, Christian Del Prete, Eve Ann Koch, and Suzanne King.

Special thanks to Ken and Marianne Turow who remain great friends and who provided me with the space to work peacefully on the original manuscript. As before, I comment that my parents, Meyer and Helen Zaremba, are to be recognized for providing me with an unusually strong foundation for life. This foundation makes it easier for anyone to do anything. I am aware of my good fortune. Thanks also to my brother, Dr. Robert Zaremba and his son Matthew, to whom this book is dedicated. Bobby and Matthew have been to me what family members should be. They are supportive and remind me of the importance of familial love for one's general mental health. Finally, I thank Donna Jean Glick, who is both my companion and, without question, my best friend.

1

Management in a New Key

AN IMPLICIT COMPONENT OF MANAGERIAL EFFECTIVENESS

In the Rodgers and Hammerstein musical, *The King and I*, the King of Siam sings the introspective soliloquy, "Tis a Puzzlement." The King is perplexed. Much of his life has become a puzzlement; he sings:

> There are times I almost think
> I am not sure of what I absolutely know...
> Very often find confusion,
> In conclusions I concluded long ago...
> In my head are many facts
> that as a student I have studied to procure...
> In my head are many facts of which
> I wish I was more certain I was sure.

Like the King, there are times when I begin to wonder about the wisdom of assumptions that long ago I had concluded to be the stuff of absolute fact. One conclusion, however, that I have never doubted is the conclusion that effective communication is an implicit dimension of effective management.

This conclusion is incontrovertible. Communication is an integral, not peripheral, factor that affects managerial success. Consequently, communication is one of the most important keys to organizational effectiveness. It is, in fact, a new key to many managers who have not or do not recognize the pervasive impact of communication on their managerial efficiency.

In the modern organization, few problems are more insidious than poor communication. One need not be a sage to recognize this or to understand why effective communication in organizations is so fundamentally important.

Organizations function by operating interdependently. Thus, the quality of communication between units, and between employees within departments, is likely to affect the quality of the corporate product. Product quality directly affects corporate profit or whatever else marks the income for a particular organization.

Poor internal communication, therefore, can quickly damage the corporate bottom line. In addition, poor internal communication can result in bruised interpersonal relationships that directly or indirectly undermine the efficiency of the organization.

In order to be effective then, managers need to manage with the understanding that communication is an important dimension of their overall job responsibilities. They must be able to manage in a new key. Without this ability, otherwise knowledgeable and skilled people are likely to become ineffective managers at best and incompetent ones at worst. There's nothing equivocal about it. "No puzzlement."

The Need for Managerial Training in Communication

Raymond Beaty is the president of Development Systems International, a management consulting firm. In a paper dealing with communication in organizations, Beaty writes

> Either through direct observation within a corporation or looking at a variety of studies which have been published, a good percentage of a manager's total behavior is some form of communication—most indicate 70-80 percent....

That's a rather high percentage. Close to four-fifths of all managerial behavior involves some form of communication. What's also telling is Beaty's contention that despite the pervasive role of communication behavior in management, most managers "have had little or no formal training or education in communication."

Such training, it seems, would have to be essential. Writing in *The New York Times*, Edward Mazze, dean of the school of business administration at Temple University, listed what he considered the ten top requisite skills for those who want to be effective in business. The number one item on Mazze's list was communication skills.

Beaty and Mazze are hardly alone in recognizing the inherent importance of effective communication in management. There are other indicators that reflect, if nothing else, a general recognition that communication is important for managerial success.

It is rare when perusing "help wanted" advertisements for management positions not to see "excellent communication skills" as a prerequisite for successful candidates. Increasingly, newspapers and business periodicals have regular sections that discuss problems related to communications. A new periodical, *Management Communication Quarterly*, is devoted solely to the subject. A number of associations, like the International Association of Business Communicators, have been formed—and have flourished—reflecting the recognition of linking communication to business.

In addition, the field has become a fertile one for knowledgeable and less-than-knowledgeable entrepreneurs. I report with some mixed emotions that there are no fewer than ninety-five firms listed in the *Boston Yellow Pages* under the heading of "Communication Consultants."

The recognition of the importance of effective managerial communication is seen on college campuses. The American Assembly of Collegiate Schools of Business (AACSB), the accrediting agency for colleges of business, has indicated that business programs must include curricula that deal with principles of communication. Throughout the nation and in increasing numbers, students are selecting courses of study that focus on issues of corporate communication.

And, of course, practitioners often refer to the importance of different aspects of communication skill for corporate success. Lee Iacocca, the organizational guru of the eighties, wrote in his autobiography, "I've known a lot of engineers with terrific ideas who had trouble explaining them to other people. It is always a shame when a guy with great talent can't tell the board or a committee what's in his head."

In an interview that appeared in the March 1988 issue of *Inc.* magazine, author and management consultant Paul Strassmann made the following comment that makes for a good concluding statement, "In the information age, all that matters is information and communication. Just remember this: Organization means communication, communication means connectivity, connectivity means knowledge. That's the mantra."

Mantra or not, the general recognition that communication is important is there. What is not there, despite all this recognition, is a tremendous amount of success in terms of implementation. What is not there is the ability to manage in this new key.

PROBLEMS WITH MANAGEMENT AND COMMUNICATION

Organizations are notorious for having poor internal communication. Michael Lobiondo, a New York management consultant, commented in the Long Island newspaper, *Newsday*, "When I go into a company the thing I most often find is that communications are very poor...You talk to several people and it's almost as if they're in different companies."

Also in *Newsday*, Maine-based consultant Walter St. John remarked, "It's fairly rare that a company has any systematic, organized communications program at all."

It is remarkable how often acquaintances have complained to me about poor communication at their place of work. At least two out of five persons with whom I discuss my work comment that their offices have extremely inefficient communication. Frequently, these people go on to discuss how such poor communication erodes morale and productivity.

This may seem contradictory. That is, if organizations recognize that internal communication is important, why are organizations not better at communicating internally? Why is it that many organizations do not place a high priority on maximizing their communication efficiency?

Despite the apparent contradiction, there are understandable reasons for inefficient communication. *In fact, it makes sense that there would inevitably be communication problems in most organizations for the following four reasons.*

Reason #1: Preconceptions, Misconceptions, and Ignorance of What Communication in Organizations Involves

Many people really do not understand what managerial communication entails. They think only of facets of communication study when they use the word "communication."

To some, communication means presentation skills. To others, communication refers to new technologies used to disperse internal information. To still others, communication may mean the company newsletter or written monthly reports. But while managerial communication includes all of this, it also transcends these narrow areas. As pundit Saul Gellerman wrote in *The Management of Human Relations*, "Communication actually consists of a great deal more than what individual managers say or information that managements publish. Corporations frequently overlook this obvious point when they attempt to improve their communication systems." For example, communication problems in organizations might involve:

- The inappropriate use of print communication. An overabundance of memos, bulletins, and internal letters.
- A hyperactive grapevine. An unusually active "informal" communication network, which spreads inaccurate information.
- A defensive communication climate, which intimidates employees and keeps them from expressing themselves without fear of retribution.
- A credibility problem within the organization that makes employees wonder about the veracity of the messages they do receive.
- A weak interoffice mail system, which results in correspondence being received late.
- An ineffective method of notifying employees of how well or how poorly they are performing. This often results in fear, mistrust, and sometimes anger toward the organization.
- Employee perceptions that no one is concerned with their suggestions and input. This results in employee reluctance to communicate to management regarding important issues that management needs to know about.

- A heavy and inappropriate reliance on committees and meetings. Meetings are not the panacea for all organizational problems and sometimes create communication problems because of overuse and/ or meeting mismanagement.
- Informational briefings/presentations that are neither informational nor brief and are perceived as time wasters by subordinates.

These are some examples of common communication problems in organizations. It is, of course, important to recognize the many facets of managerial communication. To exclude, for example, anything but improving presentational skills from the scope of the analysis is to guarantee further communication problems.

A prestigious management journal recently published an article in which the terms *communication* and *presentations* were used synonymously. Also, a successful communication consultant packages a program titled "Building Communication Skills" that is entirely devoted to improving public speaking ability. Such narrow approaches to solving communication problems will result in some more polished speakers, but also a perpetuation of continued managerial communication problems.

Reason #2: Communication is Not a Primary Activity

Workers are employed primarily to produce a quality product or service, not to produce high-quality communication. Communication may be essential to the satisfactory completion of an assignment, but communication strategy is likely to be a tertiary consideration—if it is a consideration at all.

Simply, employees are too heavily involved in their daily regimen to examine their communication styles. The architect draws. The engineer "engineers." The construction worker builds. The primary focus is on jobs themselves. When things get hectic, attention is not focused on the wisdom of different methods of message dissemination but on completing the grand product so that it can be presented at the meeting in Kansas City.

Only when a breakdown occurs do employees groan about poor communication and consider hiring a consultant or conducting a seminar to improve communication within the organization. Usually, such reactive approaches to communication problems are only band-aid solutions and do not offer anything novel. Robert Townsend was correct when he wrote in *Up the Organization*, "Management consultants are people who borrow your watch to tell you what time it is and then walk off with it."

A source of communication problems in organizations, as anyone who takes the time to look at a watch will tell you, is that communication is not a primary activity.

[In writing about communication, we refer mainly to internal organizational communication, and not public relations, advertising, and consumer affairs. Certainly there are those who are paid handsomely to communicate effectively in these areas, and we will address the distinction between internal and external organizational communication in Chapter 3.]

Reason #3: Lip Service Acknowledgments of the Importance of Communication

While many spew the appropriate utterances regarding the importance of effective corporate communication, some of these same people feel that effective employee communication ought to be "a given." That is, some managers assume that intelligent employees should, can, and will communicate effectively. This assumption is simply not true.

Intelligent, unintelligent, and semi-intelligent employees all have difficulty communicating in organizations for a variety of good reasons. To assume that communication should or will not be a problem for the otherwise competent is to decide, at least in this regard, to behave like some sort of corporate ostrich and be conveniently blind to those things that may be potentially damaging.

Reason #4: Communication Involves Sensitive Issues

Communication problems often involve issues of personality, self-esteem, and social dexterity. These are all sensitive areas. Communication problems sometimes take a back seat in organizations simply because some managers are reluctant to deal with the delicate roots of communication problems. The fragile nature of the psyche of employees and of the managers themselves makes dealing with certain issues uncomfortable.

For example, assume that at the root of a communication problem is a megalomaniacal manager who cannot bear to speak in less than a bombastic, supercilious manner. Assume that this manager adopts this condescending posture to compensate for a poor self-image. In this unfortunately not atypical case, dealing with the inevitable fallout will be difficult. Often, instead of dealing with the communication problems that surface, employees will attempt to avoid them out of concern for their own corporate survival or personal comfort.

Again, the end result of ineffective communication is not only poor product quality, but often strained employee relationships. Strained relationships beget additional communication problems and are at the root of pervasive organizational tension. Such tension can directly and indirectly affect productivity for years.

Communication and Organizational "Health"

Consider the following metaphor. Though it may appear to be extreme, the comparison is particularly illustrative and will hold up under scrutiny.

Think of communication in an organization as if it were oxygen in our respiratory systems. That is, imagine communication to be that which facilitates the physical operation of the organizational system.

Certainly, organizations with poor internal communication can "live," but like the ingestion of unclean and perhaps toxic air, the use of inappropriate and ineffective communication strategies will result in a system that does not function as well as it might. At some point, if the air is bad enough, the system might even "get sick," malfunction, and become significantly less productive. The comparison is not inappropriate. Poor internal communication can affect the fibre of the organizational foundation.

THE EVOLUTION OF COMMUNICATION STUDY IN ORGANIZATIONS

Managerial communication, as an area of study, is still in its infancy. Its development arises from the need for effective communication in business contexts. Additionally, the evolution of management theory has made it very clear that communication is a vital part of organizational health. The following changes and brief description of the developments in management theory will explain why communication is an essential part of management from a practical viewpoint, as well as a theoretical viewpoint.

The Classical Approach

The earliest theory of management, known as the Classical approach, held that employees were basically lazy people. Given the choice, employees would opt to avoid work and, generally speaking, did not enjoy working. According to Classical theorists, the way to motivate employees was to dangle a twenty-dollar bill in front of their collective noses and walk backwards. Bonuses and promises of salary increases got employees to work harder.

In addition, the Classical theorists held that employees needed the appropriate physical climate to do what was expected of them. Employees, for example, needed heat when it was winter and light when it was dark.

The Hawthorne Studies

In 1939, results from the Hawthorne Studies changed the attitudes of management theorists. The Hawthorne Studies involved the observation of employees at a Western Electric plant in Illinois. Certain employees were taken off the line and observed while researchers varied some of their working conditions. One condition that was varied was the lighting.

Initially, the researchers increased the lighting and discovered, as they suspected they might, that employees produced more of the product than they had been producing with less light. However, the researchers were stunned to discover that when the lighting was dimmed the employees continued to produce more than their normal level. At some times, the employees were practically working in the dark, yet they continued to produce more than normal.

The conclusions drawn from this research, commonly called the Hawthorne Effect, hold that employees are not motivated only by money and physical comforts but also are motivated by observation. It was clear that when people were being watched and felt that, for whatever reason, there was unusual concern for them, they became highly motivated workers.

The Human Relations Approach

Because of the Hawthorne Studies, a new approach to management theory surfaced. The Human Relations approach held that employees could find work as enjoyable as play—*given the right working environment.*

According to the theory, it was essential that employees be "stroked" and recognized for their work in ways that were not necessarily monetary. Since observation was a key motivating factor, employees needed to be made aware that their work was recognized.

The Human Relations approach, then, required effective communication. Managers needed to communicate recognition and respect to their employees.

The Human Relations approach did not work, and it did not work for a number of reasons. First of all, many managers attempting to implement the Human Relations approach came from Classical orientations and simply could not or would not effectively express recognition and concern for employee performance (or lack of performance). If a manager barks compliments at employees, the communication style will undermine the apparent content of the message. Secondly, recognition of performance cannot be doled out indiscriminately. While it is true that employees need to be told that they are appreciated, managers cannot indicate their appreciation *en masse*, because such declarations are inevitably perceived as being insincere.

We have all seen letters praising "all employees." They get copied and are nearly faded from age or too many passes through the copier. How meaningful can blanket praise be? Consider employees' reactions when they saw the following letters.

TO: All Employees

FROM: Harold Hill, The New Director of Sales and Marketing

RE: WEEK ONE

Although I have yet to meet all of you personally, please accept my sincere "thanks" for making my first week at the company an outstanding personal and business experience.

Each person I've observed has clearly exemplified the reputation I was aware the company had prior to the honor of becoming a member of the family.

I promise I will do my best to continue to maintain, cultivate, and expand on the company's tradition of excellence.

Thank you for your warm and enthusiastic welcome.

Another perennial, and equally ineffective, favorite usually takes a form something like:

Dear (insert name here):

Thank you for the great job you've done here at our corporation. Don't think for a minute that we don't appreciate what you've done for us. So to you, (insert name here), we just want to say thanks!

The Management

As Adlai Stevenson once said, "Flattery is all right—if you don't inhale." Employees can see through less-than-ingenuous praise. It's counterproductive. Every company has employees who are not deserving, and those who are, resent being packaged together with those who do not or will not produce.

A last reason why the Human Relations approach fails is because it is basically too shallow to be sound. Certainly, the Hawthorne Studies proved that employees needed to be observed and recognized, but it did not discount the fact that employees could also be motivated by monetary rewards and creature comforts. It also did not discount the possibility that some employees were indeed lazy and would delight in getting something for nothing.

The Social Systems Approach

The third school of management theory is called the Social Systems approach, and it is a hybrid of Classical and Human Relations approaches—with an important addition. According to this systems approach, organizations are seen as interdependent units that need to interact cooperatively in order to produce a high-quality product. The organization is seen as a system that exports a product or service into the outside community and relies upon the influx of money or other resources to maintain operations.

Clearly, the linkages between departments are seen as crucial in order to ensure that what is exported is likely to guarantee sufficient quantities of imported resources, such as money, to make operating the organization worthwhile.

From a theoretical standpoint, if an organization is a system, it is easy to see the need for effective communication. Simply, the left hand has to know what the right hand is doing in order for the left and right hands to work intelligently. It is not by magic that departments discover what the others are doing, although the examination of some organizations might spur some speculation.

Also, as a rule, people need human contact and recognition, not only at home but at the workplace. Therefore, it makes sense that a positive climate at work is conducive to quality productivity. The foundation of that positive climate is good interpersonal relations, and these are fostered by effective communication. This includes both effective employee communication skills and effective communication policies implemented by the organization.

The analysis of communication in organizations, then, has its roots in the evolution of management theory. It seems clear that from both an interdepartmental perspective and an interpersonal perspective, it is important to have high-quality internal communication in order to maximize organizational efficiency.

THE FUNDAMENTAL PRINCIPLE OF RECEIVER ORIENTATION

Given the importance of effective communication in the organization, the remainder of this book discusses methods that can help managers in this regard. As a foundation for that discussion, it is necessary to understand the basic communication principle of "receiver orientation."

The best way to define communication for the purposes of this book is to define it as a receiver-oriented phenomenon. This means that communication is said to have occurred when a receiver makes some sense out of a message that he or she has received.

Simply, when a message is generated, the generation in and of itself does not constitute communication. When a receiver gets the message (either correctly, or in many instances incorrectly) a message is said to have been communicated. A receiver-oriented definition not only accounts for intentionally sent messages, but also for all those times we communicate information when we have no intention of doing so.

Obviously the goal in communication, whether in organizations or in someone's backyard, is to have the desired receiver get messages accurately. In the words of Boston Celtic mentor Red Auerbach, "It's not what you tell them that's important. It's what they hear."

More about this will be discussed in the next chapter, but it is important here to state clearly that we cannot intelligently manage communication if we adopt a "sender orientation." Our focus in managing information has to be on those strategies and factors that are likely to facilitate the accurate receipt of messages generated. Only when messages are accurately received can we label our communication effective.

ELEMENTS NECESSARY FOR EFFECTIVE COMMUNICATION IN THE ORGANIZATION

The components necessary to facilitate effective organizational communication are many and complex. In order to maximize the chances for such success, managers need to:

- Consider and use various methods of sending information in order to facilitate accurate receipt.
- Cultivate and maintain viable networks that permit the flow of organizational information.
- Cultivate a supportive organizational climate that is conducive to information sending and receiving.
- Recognize the importance of nonverbal factors in determining communication success.
- Be capable of making presentations consistent with specific managerial needs.

- Be capable of interacting with employees on a comfortable, one-to-one level.
- Intelligently participate in and manage conferences and meetings consistent with specific managerial needs.

The remaining chapters deal with each of these components in detail.

2

Managing Information: Messages

On Wednesday, October 20th, David Madison received a letter through the interoffice mail. He opened the envelope and read that there would be a meeting of all budget directors to discuss changes related to company spending. The meeting would take place on the fourth floor of the Hedges building at two o'clock.

David Madison was surprised that he had received this letter, because he was not a budget director nor was he even remotely involved in financial matters. Madison did, however, get a laugh out of the mailing because when he glanced at the bottom of the letter he noticed something that was "par for the course." On this day, Wednesday October 20th, David Madison had received a notification for a meeting to be held on Tuesday October 19th.

"Very typical," thought David Madison.

Managers send and receive a great deal of information. They have to in order to meet their organizational obligations. For example, managers send information regarding departmental policies, specific work assignments, and the quality of employee performance.

As indicated in Chapter 1, the management of these messages requires care. Poor information management not only can affect the organizational product but may be damaging to employee attitudes in subtle and not-so-subtle ways. David Madison's likely reaction to the letter he received will transcend amusement. It may affect the way he views the entire organization and, perhaps, his motivation to excel within it.

This chapter deals with the subject of organizational messages and suggests approaches managers can take in order to manage information strategically. In brief, managers must understand what types of messages need to be relayed to employees and what methods are most effective in relaying this information.

Example: A Football Analogy

An aspiring football quarterback who throws a beautiful spiral pass may hear some "oohs" and "ahs" from admiring spectators, but he is unlikely to make the team unless his beautiful spirals connect with one of his receivers. That is, no matter how spectacularly esthetic a forward pass may be, it is of absolutely no use to the team unless a teammate catches the pass.

The same is true with organizational messages. Managers must recognize that the objective in managing information is to ensure that receivers get the message. Without reception, the sending of the message is meaningless.

Although managers have the same task as football quarterbacks, they are at a much greater disadvantage than their football counterparts. In football, receivers typically will do anything to catch the ball. They will dive, jump, and take two-hundred-pound insults to their bodies in order to complete a pass. Managers are not so lucky. For good and bad reasons, *corporate receivers typically do not actively pursue information.* They are often quite content to let managerial messages sail by without moving at all to "receive" the information. Even when the messages land directly in their laps, corporate receivers often expend little energy to ensure that the reception is secure.

In order to complete their "passes," managers must consider the nature of their various audiences and carefully consider what types of "passes" are likely to be caught.

FIVE ESSENTIAL CRITERIA

Not only do managers have to adopt a receiver-oriented strategy and make sure their receivers get the message, but they also have to consider the "quality" of the reception; how the message is likely to be perceived by the receiver. Some types of receptions are worse than no reception at all. Specifically, information must be:

- *Timely.* Few things are more frustrating than getting information about something that has already taken place. It is particularly aggravating to receive task-related information that does not allow enough time for the employee to complete the task.

- *Lucid.* When there is no opportunity for immediate reaction—as is the case with memos, for example—it is important that the employee be able to read the message and understand it. There is no guarantee that the employee will try to contact the source of the information if the message requires clarification. More likely, the employee will try to follow the unclear instructions and then, perhaps, make an expensive mistake.

- *Accurate.* Not only do the messages have to be clear, but the information must be correct. A clear message with inaccurate information can become a financial nightmare.

- *Pertinent.* The fact that communication in organizations is poor should not imply that there is any dearth in terms of the sheer number of messages sent to employees. Employees are swamped with messages. Irrelevant missives are often slam-dunked at orbital velocity into wastepaper baskets. It is important for employees to be aware of things that go on outside of their particular division. However, for employees to receive multiple messages requesting their presence at the meeting of all executives working on the Mercury project, when they are not executives working on the Mercury project, can be annoying and can make the employees less likely to read those messages that *are* important. If employees characteristically receive five valueless messages for every one valuable one, then the tendency might be to skim all messages and perhaps miss something important.

- *Credible.* It is important that employees believe the messages they receive and do not, either audibly or inaudibly, react to them with a sarcastic, "Sure." A history of unclear, inaccurate, or unimportant messages is likely to diminish the credibility of subsequent ones.

MESSAGE PURPOSES

Managers communicate with their subordinates, peers, and superiors for many reasons, but there are three general categories: messages regarding job tasks, maintenance messages, and human messages.

Job Task Messages

Messages regarding job tasks are those that inform employees of their specific job responsibilities/tasks. Obviously, managers need to explain to employees what they need to do and how they are supposed to do it. It may sound simple, but even the most basic task message can get distorted. Consider the following examples.

Example 1:
>   My supervisor gave me and some coworkers a specific job to do, and he wanted it done quickly. He didn't give us clear directions, however. He wanted us to carry fifty cases of soda into the walk-in cooler that was located on one side of the store. The

cooler was located directly across from a closet. Instead of telling us to put the cases of soda in the cooler, he made a mistake and, not thinking clearly, because he was busy, he said to put the soda in the closet. At first we thought it strange, but we just figured he was the boss, and left it at that. Later when he learned we did not do what he "told" us to do, he made us take everything out of the closet and put it in the cooler.

Example 2:

I work as a courier in an office building. The operation was very disorganized, and it seemed as if something was always going wrong. My worst experience with the job happened because there were two men who worked in the building by the same name of John Mederios. One John Mederios was a floor manager and the other was the editor of an organizational newsletter that came out once a week.

One day I was given an envelope and told to bring the message to a man by the name of John Mederios. I only knew one man by that name and that was the editor. I gave the editor the letter.

The message turned out to be a note to the floor manager John Mederios. The note expressed dissatisfaction with employees under Mederios's supervision. The note indicated that all of Mederios's employees should be reevaluated.

Incredibly, the Mederios editor thought the message was a "letter to the editor" intended for his newsletter and printed it in the newsletter complete with the source's name. It was a total disaster.

While the results in both cases may range from insignificant to disastrous, these both are examples of simple mistakes that can happen to anyone regardless of how intelligently communication is managed.

The following examples are different in that in each case the problem is rooted in factors that are more complex than simple confusion or improper identification. What is more, they are not particularly atypical.

The first example involves a basic task message that needed to be relayed: a manager wanted employees to clean up a store. The second example illustrates how a manager's instructions are (conveniently) misinterpreted. The third example relates to the training of a new employee.

Example 1:

I'm a salesperson, and our store recently changed managers. The replacement manager came from a different branch of the same nationwide chain. He was well experienced in management, but not in communication. For instance, I think he was intimidated by the salespeople. He is a relatively shy and quiet person, who doesn't say much—even in conversation that's not job related.

When he came to us he noticed that our store wasn't as clean as his other unit had been. He wanted to tell us about his dissatisfaction. He wanted to tell us to clean up more, but he just couldn't do it. Instead he wrote a small note addressing the problem and placed it in a very obscure place back in the office where no one on the job spends any time at all. Of course, the tidiness of the store stayed the same. I really lost a lot of respect for the new manager and I believe he turned the situation into a larger problem than it had been originally.

Example 2:

I'm a manager. About ten people work under me. On a Monday I assigned a worker to a project that absolutely had to be taken care of within a week. I explained this in detail face-to-face. I asked on a number of occasions if he understood the assignment, and I was adamant about the need for the work to be completed after the following weekend.

On Friday, this particular worker came to the office with a bad cold. He was sneezing and coughing and looked under the weather. I knew that he'd been working hard on the project so I figured if I let him go home a bit early, he could rest up and bang it out at home over the weekend when he felt better about it. People work at home all the time in this business. I told him to take the rest of the day off, but to make sure that he got the work done when he felt better. He told me "No problem" and left.

On Monday after he got settled, I asked for the completed work. He looked at me like I was crazy and said that I'd told him that he could complete it on Monday. I nearly went berserk. He saw me getting angry and said almost indignantly that I had told him that he could take the day off on Friday, so he assumed that I meant he could work on it for an extra day. I was very upset at the irresponsibility, because now I had to either go to my superior and explain why the work was late or do the whole thing myself.

Example 3:

I accepted a position as a merchandiser with a large discount department store chain. As part of my training I was to spend three weeks in a unit to "get the in-store experience." In theory, it seemed like a good idea. In reality, it was a disaster. Although the home office provided a brief outline of areas to cover, these areas could be completed in a total of about four days. The unit store manager didn't really know what was expected of him and had other things to think about so I was dumped on a few department managers and ended up spending most of the time watching videotapes and reading manuals designed to train cashiers and warehouse people— not merchandisers.

The nature of these problems is more complex. In the first example, the problem reflects a *lack of interpersonal communication skill.* The second showed a *lack of recognition* regarding how people—sometimes conveniently—process information. The third example illustrated a *lack of concern* for the importance and methods of sending information regarding job tasks. In each example, the result of the poor communication transcended the inaccurate receipt of information and resulted in negative attitudes.

Maintenance Messages

Maintenance messages deal with organizational procedural matters. Managers need to disseminate information regarding organizational policies, changes in organizational policy, and generally, information on how to proceed within the organization. Employees appreciate receiving communications regarding organizational policy and need the information to do their task-related work.

The *Employee Handbook* is a compilation of these maintenance messages. Information on shift change information inserted into pay envelopes is also an example of a maintenance message.

Whereas a maintenance message might inform employees of schedules, dress codes, sick days, and health benefits, a task message would tell employees what they had to do daily in order to fulfill their organizational responsibilities. For example, a maintenance message might be: "You must check in at nine and leave at five. There's an hour for lunch." A task message might be: "Make sure you get those employee evaluations in by next Tuesday."

Consider the following example regarding the dissemination of a maintenance message. It involves the distribution of a rules and regulation bulletin.

I work as a cocktail waitress. Right in the middle of a shift on a Saturday night my manager approached me with the new updated employee handbook of rules and regulations. He also had with him a clipboard with signatures on it. The following words were written at the top of the sheet on the clipboard.

"I have received and read my copy of the [restaurant] employee handbook, and I am fully aware of the regulations and penalties therein."

I had a whole section of people waiting for drinks and absolutely no time to read the handbook, which was about thirty pages long. I thought that since he approached me with the handbook at such a hectic time, it didn't matter that much to management whether I read the handbook or didn't read the handbook. I signed the clipboard and tossed the handbook behind the bar where it is probably still sitting. I don't know of any waitress who read it. For the most part, people just laughed when they saw it.

I think that the reason for the whole thing was to make it easier for the management to fire us if we screwed up.

It's easy to see that poor management in regard to these procedural messages can result in not only the inaccurate receipt of information but a loss of employee confidence in the entire enterprise.

Human Messages

Any message whose purpose is meeting human needs of the employees is called a human message. Something as simple as, "Hey Tom, how was your weekend?" is a human message. A formal letter thanking someone for a job well done is also an example of a human message.

These are important. Employees need recognition. They tend to work more efficiently when there is such recognition. Therefore, for this reason if for no other, human messages cannot be an afterthought and must be considered a bona fide component of managerial strategy regarding the sending of messages.

This is not to say that managers are required to coddle employees or should run around with lollipops making sure that everyone is happy. The suggestion is simply that managers should show appreciation when the situation warrants it and recognize that subordinates are human beings who need such recognition.

It is not uncommon for employees to remark that the simplest gesture of appreciation means a great deal. Faculty colleagues, for example, will often pull student notes from their desks and comment that the sentiments were as meaningful as monetary rewards. A cleaning woman said that a stuffed animal she received from a grateful administrator meant "the world to me." Everyone likes to have their work acknowledged regardless of income bracket.

One could argue that there are times when employees' needs in this area are excessive. One cannot argue, however, with the general premise that managers need to be effective sending these messages when situations warrant it.

STRATEGIES FOR DIFFUSING MESSAGES

Clearly, the dissemination of information regarding task, maintenance, and human information is an important aspect of management. How to send information to subordinates and superiors to meet these three message needs is also an important aspect.

There are various options available. Managers can write memos, phone employees, use intercoms, compile handbooks, use fax machines, use some type of video message, call a department meeting, post a bulletin, or meet with employees personally. This list in no way exhausts all possible methods for sending information within organizations. The key is to recognize that there are various methods and that there are differences between the methods. Since how information is sent may affect the nature of reception, managers need to examine the nature of the receiver or receivers and the strengths and weaknesses of each individual communication alternative.

The specific message alternatives and their advantages and disadvantages addressed in this chapter do not exhaust all the possible internal diffusion devices. They do, however, represent the most common print and electronic mass communication strategies used within organizations. (Meetings, public presentations, and face-to-face interaction will be discussed in separate chapters.)

Print Approaches

Much of what is sent downward along the formal networks in organizations is sent by way of some print strategy such as letters, handbooks, memos, company newspaper, or magazines. Among the advantages of print is that it allows for a record of the transaction to be kept. The corporate command, "Get it in writing," has been heard in organizations throughout the country, and there are obvious reasons for keeping a record of what transpires. Those who have suffered when documents have been exposed might disagree. There *are* times when keeping a record has proven to be dangerous. However, assuming that the information is not the stuff of clandestine operations, documentation is valuable and desirable.

A print mode also allows the sender the opportunity to work and rework the message until it is as clear as possible. There are no erasers on managers' tongues, and an oral faux pas cannot be eradicated by a simple, "I didn't mean that." Print allows the conscientious manager an opportunity to "get it right" to the extent that "right" can be determined.

Receivers benefit both directly and indirectly from messages received in writing. They benefit directly because a carefully worded message is easier to understand than a jumbled one. Receivers benefit indirectly because, like senders who have an opportunity to contemplate the message before sending it, receivers have an opportunity to digest the information, making it easier to put together an intelligent reply. Without that time, receivers may feel obliged or compelled to respond immediately to a sender's phoned or orally disseminated message.

Another advantage of print is that it can be relatively quick. When dealing with two hundred employees, a mass mailing would greatly expedite the process compared to the time requirements of mass phoning or face-to-face transactions. Mail can of course be delayed, but if there is only a short amount of time to reach a great many receivers, print can be relatively speedy.

Print also ensures that the same message will be sent to all receivers. This does not mean that all receivers will perceive the information similarly, but they will all be sent the same message. In personal or phone communication, the sender may abridge a message after a number of calls or simply not express it the same way to all receivers.

In brief, those who are concerned with message diffusion should recognize that print has the advantages of permanence, preparation time, relative speed, and homogeneity (that is, the same message goes to all).

The disadvantages of print, however, are also real and need to be noted. As mentioned previously, one has to be wary of messages that may be attractively designed, but not accurately received. Print has a number of drawbacks along these lines.

Print often falls victim to a phenomenon called "print overload." Because of the sheer number of messages generated, mid-level managers in particular are inundated with print messages to the extent that even the most conscientious manager may not read them all. Employees receive bulletins, handbooks, magazines, memos, company newspapers, invitations to teas, and much more. The result is predictable. The printed messages are not all read, and some carefully constructed, worded, and esthetically packaged messages are not received.

If information about an upcoming meeting is sent by a memo, and the notice is not read by a particular employee, it will matter very little if the message got to the employee quickly and was carefully planned.

Blame could be assigned by admonishing the receiver for not reading the material. The point is not to be able to identify a guilty party, however. The point is to facilitate effective communication. Employees are not necessarily irresponsible ne'er-do-wells because they do not read all printed messages. It is inevitable that print-swamped employees might not read some of what is mailed out.

A second disadvantage of printed messages has to do with the reading skills of the employees. Of course, this factor will vary depending upon the organization and the employees in the organization. Yet it is wise to consider the possibility that some employees simply cannot read or cannot read well. More importantly, it is essential to recognize the fact that some people do not like to read and, given a choice, will not read. If a message is lengthy or poorly written, it is quite possible that it will not be read even if the employees can read.

Those who work in Human Resources departments can attest to the number of employees who do not read all of their benefit packages. Almost uniformly, employees are given booklets explaining the benefits the organization provides for them. Often these booklets arrive during an information-packed orientation session, and there is simply no time to read them. Later, employees may be surprised to learn what is available to them. One can imagine the zeal with which employees approach documents that do not have such direct benefit to their monetary and physical well-being.

A third problem with print is that some senders simply do not write well. That is, no matter how diligently a manager may try to construct a written message, the document may be marred by poor spelling, syntax, and grammar. Poorly written memos can render the messages unclear or even not credible. Also, corporate writing is notorious for being laden with jargon and peculiar phrasing, which also contributes to the message possibly being unclear to the receiver. Even when the grammar is impeccable and the language jargon free, the author's style may be drab, dull, or simply not enticing to readers.

A fourth problem is that print messages do not have any visual or vocal components to assist the receivers in the perception of information. Nonverbal messages are important factors in the decoding process, and will be discussed in greater detail in Chapter 5.

Finally, print messages do not have a vehicle for direct feedback. That is, unclear messages remain unclear since the sender of the message is not physically present when the receiver gets it. Consequently, the source cannot respond to questions a receiver might have. This indirect and delayed feedback is a major problem in the use of almost all mass communication message strategies. Feedback facilitates clarification, and there just is no direct feedback when most mass communication methods, including print, are used.

Clearly, printed messages can be good, but they must be complemented by other strategies. Organizations that spend fortunes on handsome written materials must examine the purposes for preparing them. Is the purpose to have certain information on record? If the answer is yes, then print is a very good vehicle. However, if the purpose is to reach the employee, you must consider certain realities about the consumption of written material, particularly the organizational phenomenon of print overload, and recognize the necessity of complementing this strategy with other methods.

Bulletin Boards

Despite the fact that bulletin boards could be classified as a print diffusion strategy, bulletin boards are discussed separately, because they have certain unique characteristics.

Bulletin boards can provide high-quality information which can be of service to employees and those wanting to reach employees. They provide a central location for information that allows interested receivers to go to this repository of information.

There are, however, several problems. Bulletin boards are certainly repositories, but they are notorious for being repositories of all types of unnecessary information. In certain places, bulletin boards become nothing more than artistic montages of untimely, unclear, unnecessary, and often inaccurate information. Because of this, bulletin boards are often not seen as credible sources of information.

In 1993, one organization had information posted on a bulletin board which was outdated fifteen years earlier. As of this writing, that very old information remains on the bulletin board. This is an extreme situation, but if bulletin boards do not contain timely and relevant information, they are worse than valueless because they begin to taint other messages that have the same source. Additionally, valuable information that appears with valueless information is perceived as less credible and, therefore, less valuable to both receiver and sender.

A simple way to deal with this bulletin board problem is to periodically maintain the boards by having some office within the organization assigned to perform "maintenance." Rest assured that few employees will voluntarily donate their energy to be the bulletin board caretaker, but if such caretaking is part of a responsible person's reasonable job description, then that work can and should easily be done.

With a moderate amount of energy and maintenance, bulletin boards can be the credible and valuable sources of information they need to be.

Telephone

The telephone can be an effective tool for message diffusion in an organization. It has an advantage that print communication does not have in that it allows for direct and immediate feedback from the receiver. While it cannot be used in most instances to reach large audiences simultaneously, it can traverse the globe almost instantly. The telephone does not require any writing or reading skills, and its basic functions can be learned by almost anyone.

On the other hand, the telephone's ability to reach any city on the globe does not guarantee that you will be able to contact the party you wish to reach. Often, intermediaries answer telephones. Callers are often frustrated when they are told that the desired party is "at a meeting" or "out to lunch." In addition, it is common to be placed on hold for lengths of time while ostensibly being entertained by musical pablum.

The phone, simply, does not guarantee reception. One person in an organization complained that he had spent two weeks trying to reach a party in another building of the same business complex. In each instance he would leave a message for the elusive party indicating a number of good times for a return call. For two weeks he would find pink telephone messages indicating that the phantom receiver had called while the pursuer had been out.

Another negative aspect of the telephone is that the nonverbal dimensions are limited to only vocal and not visual information. This may seem like an asset at those moments when one is dressed less than conventionally, but important nonverbal aspects of the message are not available through the telephone.

Also, phone systems often fall victim to technophobia. *Technophobia* is loosely defined as a fear of technology. One might assume that technophobia is not applicable to phone usage, and for the basic phone functions, technophobia is indeed not a problem. However, many organizations have phone systems that have sophisticated capacities, such as multifunction systems that can allow conference calls, call forwarding, call transfer, automatic redialing, and number programming. For many readers this is not new information, but many people who work with these sophisticated phone systems have never taken the time to learn how to use them to maximum advantage.

A New England telephone spokesperson bemoaned the fact that his phones could do so many more things than his customers were willing to learn. The representative, who also did the customer training, was banging his fist on his desk in apparent frustration as he relayed the information. He described the comprehensive nature of the training procedure and literature on how to operate the phones, and wailed about how people still did not know how to use the system. His remarks only reinforce the contention that sophisticated and comprehensively created messages do not always guarantee reception.

In terms of technophobia, often the worst phone "culprits" are those at the highest levels of the organization. In the corridors of top administrators, one can hear executives hesitantly telling callers that "they'll try" to forward a call. The comments are made with the trepidation usually reserved for dare-devil feats.

Transferring a call on most phone systems is as simple as mechanical things can get. Yet intelligent people are sometimes reluctant to try such a basic task. Certainly, as it becomes more common for people to use the phone with all of its capacities, technophobic reactions will dissipate. For now, though, phone systems are as capable as those who are using them.

Lastly, the telephone does not typically have the permanence of printed communication. Some people do have their phone conversations taped, but these people represent a very small percentage of the total corporate population. There is a value to this lack of permanence if one does not want to have a record of the conversation. If, however, what transpires is crucial, then a phone conversation leaves a party without the proof that a printed method provides.

The phone can be a timely and valuable strategy for diffusing information, and it also can be a source of frustration. It is certainly not a cure all for all communication problems. Complementing phoned messages with other message approaches, however, is a safe way to maximize effective communication.

Public Address Systems

Public address (PA) systems are quick methods of reaching large numbers of people simultaneously. These systems have the advantage of making sure the same message is sent out to all receivers. They are quick, and therefore, timely.

The problem with PA systems is that they are often not credible. As their title suggests, PA systems are designed to reach all of the public in a given area. All of the public, however, could not possibly need the information that comes out over the PA system—at least in most instances. On mass transit systems, for example, the information that comes from the PA system is usually applicable to some, but not all, passengers. Therefore, many passengers frequently ignore the announcements, because for the most part they are not valuable to them. Consequently, there are times when messages that are relevant are ignored. Consider the following example.

In Boston several years ago a subway system—the Green Line—was forced to limit service to a stop well before the end of the line because of a problem on the track. To address the needs of the customers, the mass transit system was providing buses for all those who wanted to go further downtown. Every thirty seconds announcements boomed over the PA system informing all riders of the problem and the alternative service. These announcements did not seem to matter. Despite the announcements, hopeful passengers continued to wait for the trains. Additional passengers who had purchased tokens from indifferent MBTA employees came down the staircase and joined the numbers who awaited the next Green Line train. The recorded announcement continued to boom through the tunnels of the subway, and the riders continued to wait for the train. The waiting passengers spent their time beefing about how slow the Green Line had become. It was not until the platform became dangerously crowded that some people began to leave—less, it seemed, from the PA announcement and more, simply, because they were tired of waiting for the subway.

Public address systems also can fall victim to simple channel noise that interferes with the clear transmission of the message. Some announcers for PA systems exacerbate this problem by racing through their announcements in a manner that makes the message discernible only to those who have heard the announcement previously and do not need to hear it again.

Video

Organizations, increasingly, are using video for the purposes of training employees. The McDonald's corporation used to train employees, for example, with a variety of oral and printed training methods. Today they complement any written and oral training with videotaped instruction.

Videotape is a permanent strategy that allows the same message to be received by multiple receivers at the convenience of the receivers. This is extremely valuable. In addition, if there are parts of the instruction that are confusing, a viewer can rewind the tape and review the part that was not clear. Also, if produced well, *industrials,* as these videos are referred to, can be a palatable way for receivers to get training information. People, generally speaking, like video.

There are, however, problems with video as a message strategy, and these problems are often overlooked by those who like the medium. First, video is relatively expensive. Unless the organization has its own video production facilities in house, revising/reproducing a video training tape is more time-consuming and costly than reprinting a publication. Therefore, the value of permanence is rendered less significant if what is permanently stored on videotape is obsolete shortly after it is placed on tape, and reproduction is particularly costly.

Second, video typically directs its content to the lowest common denominator of those who will be watching the tape. If the tape is created for a heterogeneous population, the tape will probably be very slow for anyone but the duller workers. Employees of fast-food chain restaurants have commented on the simple nature of video training tapes and the problems of maintaining interest.

If the video training comes with a facilitator, the training can be supplemented with question-and-answer sessions to clarify material. Otherwise, there is no guarantee that the trainee will concentrate appropriately on the material being presented. Stories abound about employees who check into the tape room and catch some sleep while a narrator drones on about the procedure for performing corporate tasks.

Video, for those who have in-house studios, can be an effective method of training if it is accompanied by a "live" facilitator. If not, one must wonder if the strategy is likely to facilitate the message reaching the receiver. The use of video while popular, is one of those diffusion methods that may be heavier on glitz than effective communication.

Electronic Mail/Fax Machines

The computer world has, of course, revolutionized business operations. Though these changes transcend issues related to internal organizational communication, an important impact of high technology is the effect it has had on internal corporate communication. With electronic mail, people can send information to almost global audiences, and employees can receive messages instantaneously. Fax machines are truly fantastic in their capacity to send printed information anywhere. Fax sales indicate their great demand and perceived magnificence as a speedy organizational communication device. Faxes have become nearly as standard as telephones in the business office. Business cards often contain phone, fax, and e-mail addresses. There is growth and even newer communication technology yet to come.

Fax machines and other methods of electronic message transmission can certainly be boons to internal communication in terms of the rate of message flow. However, one must be careful not to be wowed by the speed of the technology. There are problems with relying solely on electronic transmission, or perceiving fax machines, for example, as panaceas for organizational communication problems. Fax machines are magnificent in what they can do, yet their existence certainly does not eliminate all sources of communication breakdown, many of which have little to do with speed of transmission or sophistication of technology. Speed and sophisticated technology alone cannot reduce all communication problems.

There is a tendency to assume that buying a fax machine or implementing an electronic communication network will guarantee effective internal communication. It will not. Interestingly, whenever I provide a case to seminar participants that involves poor internal communication, the participants almost invariably suggest the purchase of some sort of electronic machine (usually a fax) and an increase in the use of departmental meetings as the solutions to the problem. The advantages and disadvantages of meetings will be discussed in Chapter 8, but for this chapter it's important to note that electronic strategies can't do it all.

In and of itself, high technology will not eliminate communication problems any more than the telephone eliminated all communication problems. The problems cited in the beginning of this chapter, for example, would have existed regardless of technology. In fact, as Paul Strassmann commented in *Inc.* magazine, "Technology can help deal with [management] problems, but more often than not [technology] is used to proliferate them." (For more on this, see "Technology and Quality Communication" in Appendix C on page 140.)

In concluding this section, it is necessary to emphasize the importance of complementing message diffusion strategies. Simply generating a printed memorandum does not negate the need for an additional phone call to supplement the memo. It is not a matter of coddling employees; it is a matter of recognizing the realities of message transmission in the organization. It is also necessary to emphasize that the key to effective message sending is recognizing that reception is the objective of any communication activity.

SERIAL DISTORTION

I work for a large paint company. At one point the organization advertised an incentive plan for employees. The plan called for monetary rewards to those who sold the most paint and paint accessories. In addition to salary increments, prizes like television sets and stereos would be distributed to employees who were successful at selling.

Although this promotion had the potential to be a big success, it was not, due to the fact that the information never reached the employees. My manager had received a newsletter explaining the incentive program, but had failed to relay the information to the salespeople or post the newsletter where it could be read by employees.

Regardless of whether the messages are task, human, or maintenance, they often are not perceived by receivers in the manner they had been designed to be received. Sometimes the reasons for the inaccurate reception of information are as much a function of the serial nature of communication in organizations as the particular method of diffusion employed.

Messages in organizations are typically relayed serially. That is, often there are stopping points between the original source of the message and the desired receiver of the message.

For example, a message intended for all employees in an engineering division might emanate from a chief executive officer. The message might be orally diffused at a meeting of the CEO and all organizational vice presidents. The appropriate vice president might phone the department head and ask the department head to relay the information to the employees. The department head might write a memorandum to be distributed to all employees.

Such serial transmission can result in distortions that go beyond those that occur when children engage in the game "Telephone." Some distortions may, as is the case in the Telephone game, be caused simply because of the frequency of coding and decoding. However, some distortions occur because of reasons that are related to organizations and the relationships that develop within organizations.

There are four categories of these types of distortions, some of which overlap.

Adding

Adding takes place when an intermediary adds more information or verbiage to the original message. This occurs simply because some people are more verbose than others. The human message, "Tell Harry he's a good worker," changes meaning when an intermediary writes a lengthy message congratulating Harry on work well done and suggests in the mailing that there might be a monetary reward forthcoming.

Levelling

Levelling is the opposite of adding. In levelling, the intermediary shortens the message. This can be caused because intermediaries are terse, or because of strained relationships. Assume a supervisor sends the following memo to a department head:

TO: West
FROM: King
RE: Immediate need for repair work

Unfortunately, I will have to ask you to inform John Morgan that he'll need to fix all the terminals on the sixth floor by next Wednesday. I realize this is an unusual request and does not give Mr. Morgan adequate time. However, we need these terminals repaired for the special project that we'll be embarking on in the near future. Please relay to Mr. Morgan our apologies for this short notice, but tell him it's for the company's benefit and that sometime in the future he'll be rewarded for his hard work which, by the way, we already know is of unusual quality.

Assume that the department head, West, is a taciturn sort or someone who is jealous of John Morgan because King has recognized Morgan's good work. The department head might call Mr. Morgan over and say, "Fix the terminals on the sixth floor, Morgan, and have it done by Wednesday. Orders from King. Get to it and no complaints, please."
    The above is a considerably truncated version of the original message. The content of the message may be consistent with the original; the tone however is not. Certainly, King's message has been aborted. Certainly, Morgan would have received a different message from the original than from the levelled version.

Sharpening

Sharpening refers to distortions that occur when intermediaries make information they are relaying more sensational than the news needs to be.
    Assume that Richard Duncan, a middle manager, receives a phone call from his supervisor, Jane McCoy. McCoy tells Duncan that two workers will

have to be temporarily laid off due to some budget cuts. McCoy gives Duncan the names of the two employees who will be laid off and asks that Duncan take care of the matter immediately.

Duncan calls a meeting of his employees and somberly informs the group that two people will have to be temporarily laid off. Duncan, concludes his speech with the following: "Right now it's only two. Who the hell knows what's going to be? Times are tough. This could be the start of something big. I get the feeling that heads could roll. Don't buy a new house."

I have found in my work in organizations that certain people enjoy being the bearer of startling news—as if the emotional reaction from those being startled provides some sort of payoff for the sender. Obviously the reaction to the sharpened message in the example cited above would be different from the original message.

Assimilating

Messages are assimilated when the intermediary alters the message to make it more palatable to the person who is to be the recipient of the message. This is a very common kind of serial distortion. Few people like to convey devastating news to individuals. Some may want to startle groups, but it's no fun to tell a friend or even an acquaintance that a superior is furious with performance or that employment is terminated.

If told to relay such negative messages to individuals, it's not unlikely for people to try to make the message more palatable to the receivers. For example, consider the directive:

> Tell Anderson that one more mistake like that and he is no longer working for our company. I mean it. I cannot tolerate that kind of mistake. There is no room in this organization for shoddy work. Make sure you tell him that. There's something in me that says get rid of him right now, but I'll give him one chance. I am so furious with him, I could scream. No more nonsense from him, or he gets the boot. Make sure he gets the message. You got that?

If assimilated, the message may be conveyed like this:

> The boss was unhappy about last week. You know. He was hot. He'll get over it, trust me. It's no big deal, but I just wanted you to know that he registered some concern when we last met. Don't worry about it. Let's just be more careful next time.

Serial distortions—levelling, adding, assimilating, and sharpening—are prevalent within organizations. When possible, avoid diffusing messages serially. That is, when possible communicate directly with the eventual receivers. When it is not possible to do so, try to limit the number of serial intermediaries who might distort the message.

3

Communication Networks

In order to drive from one place to another, motorists need highways. Without Interstate 90 or other alternate routes, it would be difficult to drive from Chicago to Buffalo. It does not matter whether motorists drive beat-up Chevys or Porsches, they still would have trouble getting to Buffalo by car if there are no viable routes.

Similarly, organizations require routes to facilitate the transportation of information. Managers must create, cultivate, and nourish these networks in order to permit the flow of information.

These networks do not refer to communication methods like using interoffice memos, meetings, or video training tapes. These examples are analogous to the Chevys and Porsches that use the highways. The networks refer to the highways themselves. The networks refer to the existence of navigable channels that permit the use of message strategies. The roads have to be open before motorists can use them.

To some, the distinction between networks and message strategies may seem to be minor and not particularly functional. The distinction, however, is not academic. There is a basic difference between message strategies and communication networks. To illustrate this, analyze the following two examples. The examples illustrate that the root of the communication problems in both cases is not the method of sending information but the absence of any way for important messages to get from one place to another within the organizations.

Example 1: Buckley, Marshall, and Keyes

John Buckley, a newly hired middle manager, noticed that his department was wasting a great deal of money. Since he had worked in a similar capacity previously, he was aware of a cost-saving method for production that would reduce expenditures by thirty percent.

Buckley was excited by the prospect of contributing to the department so early in his tenure and was also eager to improve his own personal stock with his superiors. He went to his immediate supervisor with the suggestion and was informed that such changes were out of her hands. It seemed as if the only person who could authorize that type of move was a vice president named Marshall.

Buckley went to make an appointment to see Marshall and was told by Marshall's assistant, Keyes, that as a general rule Marshall did not meet with middle managers. Buckley tried to impress upon Keyes the importance of a meeting with Marshall, but Keyes insisted that no interviews would be granted and became annoyed at Buckley's tenacity.

Buckley did not give up. He wrote a three-page explanation of the cost saving measure and sent it to Marshall through interoffice mail.

Two weeks later, after hearing nothing, he phoned Marshall and was intercepted by the assistant, Keyes. Buckley inquired about the proposal and was told, peremptorily, that Marshall was a very busy person and it was unlikely that the proposal would be reviewed in the near future.

Buckley discovered afterwards that Marshall's mail was always read by the protective Keyes and that it was unlikely that Marshall had ever received the proposal. At this point he decided to forget the matter. His enthusiasm faded to indifference. "Let the company continue to lose money," he thought. "It doesn't matter to me."

Example 2: The Edison Records

A retail record and tape company sold records, tapes, and audio accessories out of several retail outlets as well as through mail order. The mail order division had a sales department, a billing department, and a credit department that pursued customers with bad debts.

A Mr. Edison purchased two records via mail order and received the merchandise and billing simultaneously. He played the records upon receipt and discovered that one record was damaged. He proceeded to send a package by mail to the company. In the package he placed the damaged record, the original order form, a check for the good record, and a simple note requesting a replacement copy for the defective product. On the note, Edison indicated that he would pay for the defective record when he received the replacement.

Two weeks later, Edison received a second bill from the company with "Second Notice" stamped on the form. The bill contained a placating message that read, "If you've already paid your bill, please disregard this message." Edison assumed that the sales office would soon be in contact with the billing department and did nothing. This assumption proved to be incorrect. Three days went by and Edison received a package from the record company. In the package Edison found another copy of the good record he had previously received, two copies of the defective record he had returned for replacement, and a bill for the three records.

Edison rifled a letter to the company indicating that he had not wanted to order two copies of the damaged record and that he had no use for another copy of the record that had arrived in good shape. The letter was caustic, and Edison demanded that the matter be cleared up immediately.

Ten days later Edison returned from work to find a "Third Notice" billing from the company for the original order and a Second Notice billing, (complete with placating message) for the second package he had received.

With the Third Notice in his angry fists, Edison got into his car and drove to the nearest retail outlet of the record company. He approached the manager and demanded immediate intervention.

The manager told Edison that the retail outlets had absolutely nothing to do with the mail order division and that there was no way the manager could or would communicate with the mail order people. If Edison wanted to resolve the matter, he was told, he would have to write to the mail order division directly.

Edison asked for a phone number, and he was told again that the retail outlets had nothing to do with the mail order division. Edison attempted to get a phone number for the mail order warehouse through the telephone directory and was unsuccessful.

One more time Edison wrote to the mail order division explaining the situation. He did not receive any more records. He did receive a letter from the credit department, however, indicating that his "case" had been brought to the attention of that department for appropriate action. The letter was admonishing and sternly warned of repercussions if the matter was not addressed immediately.

It took Edison three months to straighten out the situation.

During the course of Edison's investigation, he discovered that there was very little interaction between the sales, billing, and credit division. They perceived themselves as autonomous units within the larger organization and there were no systematic channels available to facilitate the movement of information on matters like his problem. Simply, the left hand did not pay much attention to what the right hand was doing.

The Edison and Buckley cases are, unfortunately, not uncommon situations. Organizations must be concerned with developing channels that facilitate the flow of information. The Edison case, especially, is so typical that it is doubtful that many readers would not have experienced a similar situation as consumers. Edison, in fact, got off easy. It can take more than three months sometimes to sort out similar confusion.

Because we are aware of the frustrations that Edison experienced—we have probably experienced them as consumers—it makes sense as managers to recognize the problem and take proactive measures to eliminate the chance that we will alienate our own clients in the same way that Edison was alienated. The Edison matter could have been easily remedied if the organization had a system of networks connecting the different units of the organization.

THREE NETWORK CATEGORIES

There are three basic network systems that operate within an organization: external and internal, formal and informal, and upward/downward and horizontal.

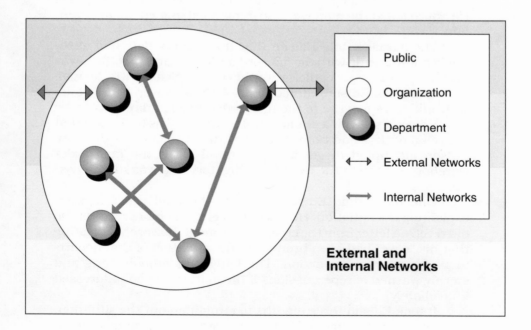

	Public
	Organization
	Department
	External Networks
	Internal Networks

External and Internal Networks

EXTERNAL AND INTERNAL NETWORKS

In organizations *external networks* refer to those channels that carry information from within the organization to outside the organization, or those networks that carry information from outside the organization to inside the organization.

Typically, external networks carry advertising messages, messages related to public relations, and messages relaying information about consumer complaints, concerns, and recommendations. External organizational communication networks have been studied more extensively than internal organizational communication networks under the headings of Public Relations and Advertising.

As is the case with most organizational interaction, there is an interdependent relationship between the external and internal networks. Consider the next example, which illustrates how poor internal management can affect the functioning of the external network.

A student intern, Stuart Markwardt, was working in the public relations department of a large high-tech company in Boston. Interns were favored by this company because, frequently, high-tech magazines would call in need of information for articles regarding new products. The high-tech public relations department was understaffed and swamped with these phone calls. Since most of the time these callers asked simple questions that any employee with some information about the organization could answer, the student interns satisfied a real need for the department.

On a particularly busy day, a writer for a nationally known financial periodical phoned, because she wanted to do a story about a new word-processing package that had recently been introduced. The full-time employee she reached was swamped with work and passed the writer along to Markwardt.

Markwardt took the call and answered the journalist's questions. At the end of the interview the journalist asked for, and was given, Markwardt's name.

Three months later, the magazine came out with a positive review of the new product. The review concluded with the information that Stuart Markwardt was the product manager for the new software product and the contact person for questions regarding the product. This, of course, was not true, but to the more than 700,000 readers of the magazine it certainly seemed like Markwardt was the person to call with questions.

By the time the article was published, Stuart Markwardt was back in school and no longer working for the corporation. Nevertheless, the company received hundreds of phone calls from persistent customers who insisted on speaking to Stuart Markwardt and no one else. Some people will not settle for second fiddle and would not be put off in their quest and clamoring for Markwardt.

The company president was flabbergasted. After he read the article he allegedly shouted, "Who is this guy, Markwardt? What the hell's a Markwardt anyway? I don't remember us hiring any Stuart Markwardt."

One year later, the company was still getting phone calls and letters addressed to the intern. Over 2,000 calls have come in asking for Stuart Markwardt. More importantly, nothing has been done to improve the external networks in order to keep such an event from happening again. That is, there are still occasions when those who are not entirely knowledgeable respond to callers who inquire about new products.

Internal Networks

Any channels *within* the organization that carry information are called *internal networks*. This can refer to intradepartmental routes and interdepartmental routes.

The systems theory of organizations described in Chapter 1 suggests the necessity for organizations to establish channels for interdepartmental interaction. If an organization is a system with interdependent parts, the organization must have a way to link the interdependent parts. As was the case with Mr. Edison and the record company, the lack of such conduits can result in customer frustration.

Often the internal channels exist, but are crudely constructed and therefore impede traffic, as was the situation with Buckley. Organizations have traditionally spent little time engineering the internal networks and ineffective internal communication is an inevitable result.

FORMAL AND INFORMAL NETWORKS

Formal networks are those that are prescribed by the organization. These are the official, appropriate channels for people to go through when relaying information. Most often these official channels have not been prescribed or described as "communication networks." They have come to be the appropriate channels, because they conform to the corporate organizational chart. These charts indicate who is to report to whom, and what the appropriate chain of command is in an organization.

The fact that a network is a formal network does not guarantee that communication "traffic" can utilize the particular channel, however. In the Buckley case, for example, Buckley was supposed to see Marshall, but he had to go through Keyes to do so. Keyes proved to be an unyielding roadblock.

To continue the highway metaphor, there are roads that appear to exist on a highway map, but for sometimes curious reasons, these roads are closed to motorists. Similarly, there are networks that appear to exist on the organizational chart, but these networks are in actuality closed to subordinates or organizational peers. Of course, there are times when "roads" might have to be closed. Vice presidents cannot be at everyone's beck and call. However, if the formal policy implies that a network is supposed to be open, it can be frustrating not to be able to ever use that network. If the organizational policy is that the conduit is simply superficial and as a practical matter is not available, the company runs the risk of not getting some valuable information.

Managers need to make sure that the formal networks are indeed available for the sending and receiving of organizational messages.

Informal networks are those channels that carry information on routes that are not prescribed by the organization. Typically, these informal routes are referred to as the grapevine, and for a number of reasons the grapevine is an important network. Managers need to know about the development, traffic, speed, accuracy, resilience, and management of these informal networks.

Development of Informal Networks. By definition, the grapevine is not prescribed. While prescient managers might attempt to engineer its development, the informal networks usually generate on the basis of factors that are only peripherally related to corporate policy.

The nature of the grapevine will be affected, for example, by the physical layout of the buildings and offices within the buildings. If production and advertising share a common lounge area and restroom facility, it is likely that an informal network will develop among those people who populate the departments of production and advertising.

Common hobbies and activities play a large part in the development of the grapevine. If seven employees from different departments jog together at lunch, information is likely to be passed along in the course of the run. The friendships that develop because of the common activity will result in social gatherings outside of the organization during which information about the organization will be passed along as well. If Smith in Production wants to find out about a policy in Engineering, Smith may not call the Engineering manager as prescribed on the formal network but contact Jones, his jogging buddy.

It is not difficult to enumerate the factors that contribute to the growth of this important network. Lunch schedules, family ties, social relationships, and common hometowns can affect the growth of the network. Even the formal network can affect the growth of the informal network. If you participate on a committee and in the course of your conference sessions become friendly with a person who previously had been a stranger, that budding friendship creates a part of the informal network.

Traffic, Speed, and Accuracy. Many messages travel along the grapevine and do so very quickly. Information moves much more quickly on the grapevine than it does on the formal network.

The existence of the grapevine and its innate speed can pose some serious organizational problems. Rumors spread quickly, and inaccurate incendiary news can move throughout a large organization in hours. Incorrect information is tough to stall once it begins to travel on the informal networks. As the British politician James Gallagher once said, "A lie can be halfway around the world before the truth has its boots on."

Although the grapevine can and does distort information, the grapevine can be and often is a rapid conveyor of accurate information as well. Often this accurate grapevine information reaches its destination before the chugging formal network can relay the message. The obvious result is employee anger and organizational embarrassment.

Managers are occasionally placed in positions where they have to deny the accuracy of information employees have received via the grapevine until such time as the formal networks, dawdling along at a glacier-like pace, can officially inform the receiver of the information. Because of the swiftness of the informal network, the relatively slow formal network, and the occasional denials issued until the formal network catches up with the grapevine, the credibility of the formal network and those who operate it can be damaged.

Resilience. It is important to remember that the grapevine is not only fast and often accurate but that it exists willy-nilly. No amount of plumbers units, directives from on high, or threats will stop the informal network from operating. As long as there are cocktail parties, racquetball courts, lunch-room cafeterias, water coolers, bathrooms, coffee machines, two chairs in an office, and sexual energy—and you can safely assume that most of these things will not go out of style soon—there will be informal networks. Therefore, managers must try to manage the informal network and not attempt to eliminate it. The latter is only an exercise in frustration.

Management. Managing the informal network is difficult. The tendency is to want to eliminate the grapevine, because the grapevine is so troublesome. Its very existence makes it difficult for employers to manage information diffusion. There often are attempts to formalize all communication travel to eliminate the informal network. I emphasize the futility of trying to uproot the grapevine. It either will not work, or it will not work for long. You may be able to fight City Hall, but you cannot fight the inevitability of human nature.

Although the grapevine, and the problems endemic to the grapevine, are realities, there are ways to deal with them. The most intelligent way is to adopt a proactive communication policy that will decrease the problems that an unwieldy grapevine can cause. The following will be helpful for grapevine management.

- *Use the informal network* . The informal networks do work. Use them. The suggestion here is not to start wild rumors but to complement the usage of the formal networks with the informal network, when appropriate.

- *If possible, be candid about information.* An organization that has a reputation for honesty makes it easy on itself. The informal network will still operate and rumors will still spread, but disclaimers can help to squelch the spread of inaccurate information if those disclaimers are believed. Of course, there are items that cannot become public information. There is nothing wrong in explaining that certain pieces of information will be diffused when the time is right for that information to be diffused. Organizations that are credible are likely to have patient employees who will believe that information will be forthcoming at appropriate times. (See Chapter 4 for more on the issue of organizational credibility.)

- *Screen employees effectively.* This point will also be addressed in greater detail in Chapter 4, but it is relevant here. The informal network will exist no matter what. If there is a garrulous employee in an important position, however, the grapevine will become unnecessarily active.

> A man named Starr was an upper-echelon administrator in a large organization. Starr was notorious for not being able to keep anything quiet. He would approach relative strangers, look both ways as if he was looking for KGB agents, and whisper, "Just between you, me, and the wall pole, Charlie Harris will be the next plant manager."

The irony in this situation was that the information that Starr often passed along, was common knowledge, yet he wanted to be in a position to relay what essentially was gossip. As one could predict, the managers who were subordinate to Starr could not believe much of what he told them and were very reluctant about passing anything up to Starr that was at all confidential.

- *Admit mistakes quickly.* Former President Richard Nixon's eventual downfall was his inability to admit mistakes. The only people who should deny mistakes are those who make such mistakes habitually. Good people will err occasionally, and admitting them is a positive trait.

The informal network is going to exist. The nature of the information that travels on the grapevine does not necessarily have to be counterproductive. There will be problems, but these suggestions can diminish the problems that the grapevine may cause.

UPWARD/DOWNWARD AND HORIZONTAL NETWORKS

Messages in organizations, whether they are formal or informal, travel in one of three directions. Either the messages travel *upward* from subordinate to superior, *downward* from superior to subordinate, or *horizontal* between employees on the same level.

Upward Networks

Without question, the formal channels that are used the least are those that carry messages from subordinate to superior. Even when these networks exist, they often are spurious.

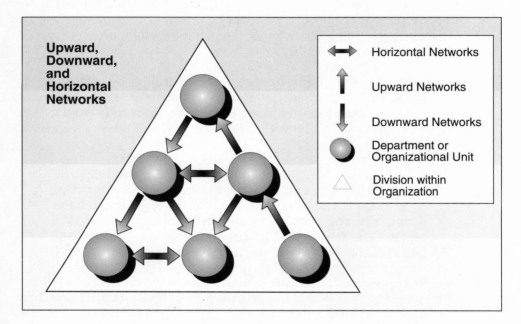

Upward, Downward, and Horizontal Networks

⬌ Horizontal Networks

⬆ Upward Networks

⬇ Downward Networks

⬤ Department or Organizational Unit

△ Division within Organization

That is, often the upward communication routes are designed to give the appearance of an existing channel for subordinate-to-superior communication, but in reality the routes are bogus or are used infrequently. This reality presents an insidious problem for management, because the upward networks are very important to the organization. The damage may not be noticed immediately, but it will eventually surface. If administered effectively, however, these upward channels would carry valuable information from subordinates to superiors.

Consider the following example, which took place within a federal agency. It is a prime example of poorly designed and managed upward networks.

One day, all the employees of this federal agency received the same letter. It was hand-delivered by their immediate supervisors. The letter indicated that a fifty-dollar reward would be offered to any employee who could present an idea to management that subsequently would be implemented by the organization.

One new employee received the letter and immediately began to contemplate a series of fifty-dollar checks being made out in his name. The employee could think of dozens of organizational problems and saw this as an opportunity to make some reward money and also to impress management. Almost immediately, he began scrawling down ideas that he intended to refine and later submit as recommendations for his reward.

A veteran of the agency watched this scenario unfold and while the newcomer feverishly scrawled, the old timer issued the following advice: "Make sure you put that idea on a soft piece of paper."

The newcomer was surprised, but continued writing. Again came the warning, "Make sure you put it on a soft piece of paper." Again, the new employee paused only momentarily from the lists. Finally, there was a third, "Make sure you put it on a soft piece of paper."

"Okay," said the kid, "Why should I put it on a soft piece of paper?"

"Cause that way," said the old timer, "it won't hurt so much when they tell you to shove it."

The kid was momentarily stunned by this earthy advice. He began to ask around and discovered that the organization issued similar "calls for suggestions" on an annual basis. However, no one could identify a single employee who had ever received any monetary reward for any idea submitted. The grapevine information was that no one even read the suggestions. Requests for suggestions were issued to create an illusion of participatory decision making, but it was nothing short of a ruse.

Any such bogus attempt will not only retard the flow of information in the subordinate to superior network, it will also help demoralize the workforce.

When talking about these channels, it is important to understand the specific values of upward networks, the problems related to creating genuine upward networks, and ways to manage and implement the upward network. As mentioned, managers need these upward channels. They are very important for a number of reasons. Upward networks allow the employees to feel like they are part of the company; as if they have "a piece of the rock" and their opinions matter. This opportunity, all other things being equal, is likely to improve morale.

In addition, subordinate-to-superior networks provide a vehicle for obtaining feedback for messages that have been sent downward. When a superior sends a message to subordinates, that superior should want to get some reaction. Subordinate-to-superior communication networks facilitate the acquisition of this feedback.

People on lower levels of the organization are often aware of problems that people on the top levels of the organization could not possibly be privy to. If a machine is malfunctioning on a certain level, it might take an unnecessarily long time for that malfunction to come to the attention of the appropriate manager, if not for a subordinate-to-superior network.

Employees may have suggestions that can be valuable for the organization. Reportedly, the American phenomenon, Egg McMuffin, and all of that sandwich's clones, originated from an idea generated by a lower level McDonald's employee. The employee commented that the sandwich was delicious, and that the company ought to try it as a breakfast fare offering.

Finally, subordinate-to-superior networks can be valuable because employees on different levels of the organization have specialized knowledge and expertise. It is in the best interest of the organization to allow this esoteric knowledge to be ventilated to upper management. Even the brightest manager is unlikely to know as much about a particular operation as that person who performs that operation daily. It is wise to solicit and tap the knowledge that is available from knowledgeable employees.

Despite the value of upward communication networks, a common and valid complaint among employees is that there are not appropriate vehicles available to carry messages from subordinate to superior. Once again, upward communication networks are rarities and are often spurious when they do exist. This is due more to human nature than to ignorance of the value of these networks.

People, no matter who they are and no matter how strong they might be, are reluctant to solicit rejection. When managers use the upward network, they invite criticism. Occasionally, that criticism will not be constructive. Sophomoric and destructive criticisms may surface only once in a great while, but they will still be painful regardless of their relative infrequency.

For example, department heads in many organizations are required to solicit evaluations from their subordinates. After reading many positive comments, these managers are still bothered when they read caustic negative comments. They would be less than human to react differently. After reading a particularly vitriolic comment, it is unlikely that a manager will say philosophically, "Well this troubled employee represents a mere .05 percent of the subordinate population. I shall not concern myself with this silly and apparently bitter comment."

Likewise, if top management solicits recommendations and encourages suggestions from subordinates, these managers will run into similar problems. Imagine a manager reviewing a number of subordinate recommendations:

> There are not enough tables for us to work at over in engineering. More work space would be helpful. It is, it would seem, a minor investment and it would improve not only productivity, but morale as well.

The manager might react to this message by thinking, "I didn't realize there was a problem with inadequate table space. How come I wasn't aware of this? I'll check on the cost of getting more tables, and contact Davis to see if this could be done. This idea of encouraging subordinate input is a good one." The manager continues to review the recommendations:

> We would appreciate more meaningful and frequent evaluative sessions. As it is, and I think I speak for many, we often don't

know how top management is reacting to our work until it is too late. Also, the evaluations we do have seem to be meaningless formalities. Thank you.

Again the manager might think that this entire process is a good idea. The manager may decide not to do anything about the particular evaluation issue but may discuss the matter with others. At the very least, the manager has learned something that could, at some point, be important for the health of the organization. The manager picks up the third recommendation and reads:

You are the worst kind of human vermin. In addition, you run this place like some kind of Napoleonic tyrant. You think you're a class act, but I assure you that there is nothing and no one that I disrespect more. Thanks for making my life miserable.

Even though this comment might be the only one of its kind in the entire pile, it may be difficult for the manager to continue to think of soliciting subordinate recommendations as a good idea. In fact, the manager may want to know who wrote the "suggestion" and attempt some type of retribution. The manager might disregard the legitimacy of the other suggestions because of this caustic one, or the manager may try to purge the negative comment from the other comments and suggestions fearing that it could besmirch the manager's status if someone else were to come across it.

The simple reason for the under-use of upward communication networks is that few people like to hear bad things. There is a basic self-defense mechanism that operates, and there is the concomitant feeling of, "If they knew what I know, they'd be where I am."

Two employees, Barker and Walsh, worked in an office of communication of a large organization in the Northeast. The organization was having some communication-related problems and, therefore, Barker and Walsh sought the assistance of two communication researchers. Barker and Walsh wanted to know why communication was so poor in their division and why morale was so low.

The researchers listened to the managers describe their situation and then went ahead and designed a questionnaire that attempted to discover employees' attitudes toward various communication products, such as newsletters, company magazines, and corporate memos.

When the questionnaire was completed and presented to the managers, Barker and Walsh immediately requested that certain questions be purged from the survey. Not coincidentally, Barker and Walsh requested the elimination of all questions pertaining to anything that Barker and Walsh were directly responsible for.

The questionnaire contained very basic questions asking all employees within the division to comment on the quality, quantity, and need for certain communication-related efforts. Barker and Walsh, however, did not want to discover what the employees thought of their work.

Moreover, they did not want their supervisors to find out what other employees thought of their work. The researchers balked at Barker and Walsh's request to purge the potentially embarrassing questions. The researchers, then, were asked to discontinue their efforts.

Despite the fact that it is understandable that people are reluctant to use upward communication networks, these networks need to exist and need to be managed well. One way to provide this feedback without incurring the wrath or damaging the ego of an upper-level manager is to use intermediaries whose job it is to solicit upward messages and digest these messages for consumption by upper management. Certainly, such intermediaries can distort the information, and that is a problem with this intervention strategy. Upper-level managers must make a commitment to discourage such convenient digestion and not, as a matter of policy, "kill the messenger."

Managers have to remember that most messages are not vitriolic and that they indeed need these subordinate-to-superior messages. If a small percentage of the messages are nasty, an intermediary can report that there are a few complaints and some malcontents, but that most of the comments are not charged. If most of the messages are disparaging, then an intelligent manager must be able to grit some teeth and smell the coffee. It is relatively easy to do this if the messages are digested to remove the vitriol but not the essence of the content.

The point is that this subordinate-to-superior network is extremely important for organizational health, and it is an aspect of communication that however difficult, must be dealt with to improve the functioning of the organization.

If the upward networks are suggestion systems of any sort, the network should meet four specific criteria. The program should have:

- Support from top management.
- A program administrator who has this responsibility as a primary or sole job responsibility.
- Efficiently communicated instructions regarding the procedures, rules, and rewards.
- Timely and meaningful feedback for all those who participate in the program.

Downward Networks

The downward networks are the channels that are most likely to be formalized. They carry a great deal of the official superior-to-subordinate information. Formal downward networks travel relatively slowly.

It is important to emphasize that downward networks tend to be "one-way streets." Messages sent along the downward networks are only valuable if they reach their destinations. As one-way streets, downward networks are not conducive to facilitating feedback. Senders often do not know if information they sent was received or how it was received.

Certainly, information has to travel downward, but what is the use of the voyage if the information winds up in a cul de sac and the source is not aware of it. Obviously, downward networks must be utilized in conjunction with upward networks. If communication has as a goal the accurate receipt of information, sending information downward must have some mechanism for feedback.

Horizontal Networks

Horizontal networks transport information along the same strata of an organization. Formal horizontal networks are rarities, particularly at the lower levels of the hierarchy. Top managers may meet periodically to discuss the nature of each manager's division. At the lower levels, however, employees are unlikely to have any formal horizontal contacts.

Because of this, information that gets relayed from peer to peer (interdepartmentally, not intradepartmentally) in an organization often takes a circuitous route. For example, members in a production department who need information from the engineering department may get this information in the following way.

The engineers may have a departmental meeting discussing a new project. The department head might meet with her supervisor as part of a regularly scheduled conference and relay information about the new project. The supervisor may meet with all department supervisors once a week and convey information about engineering's new project at this weekly meeting. The supervisor in charge of the production department might phone the department head of production explaining the engineering project. The department head might relay the information to the production employees.

The information, obviously, is taking the scenic route. Because of this indirect routing, information can be lost, distorted, or arrive too late. Therefore, it is a good idea to design and formalize horizontal networks for message flow, particularly between departments that work on matters of direct mutual importance.

4

Managing the Communication Climate

A professor at Purdue University and a pioneer in the field of organizational communication, W. Charles Redding made the following comment about organizations, communication, and the organizational climate in his book, *Communication Within the Organization*:

> The climate of the organization is more crucial than are communication skills or techniques (taken by themselves) in creating an effective organization.

Redding is, of course, correct. More important than individual employees' communication skills is the atmosphere within which individual employees interact. If an organization employs five hundred people and all of these employees have excellent communication skills—that is, they can speak, write, and listen well—it will matter little if the workplace has an unpleasant atmosphere that discourages interaction.

All but the charmed reader can recall jobs where the communication climate within the organization militated against effective receipt of information. Perhaps it was some ornery supervisor, belligerent coworker, or defiant subordinate that contributed to the problem. Perhaps it was simply a system that cultivated defensiveness. Whatever it was, your eloquence or willingness to listen meant very little. The defensive climate undermined your potential and the organization's potential.

Make no mistake about it. Do not delude yourself into thinking otherwise. The organizational climate is the single most important variable in determining the quality of managerial communication. Cultivating and/or maintaining a supportive climate is the essential initial step for any manager who is interested in managing in a new key.

No expensive seminar on conference communication, no series of lectures on listening skills, and no external training consultant to improve presentations will be valuable unless the organization has a supportive climate.

Creating the supportive climate, however, is an extremely difficult task, even for the most personable and diligent manager. It is certainly much easier to enumerate the characteristics of supportive climates than to generate them. Consider the list below of some of the trademarks of supportive climates:

- Manager/subordinate trust and respect
- Nondeceptive, honest communication
- Participatory decision making
- A team atmosphere

While these are legitimate elements of supportive climates, they are at the same time extremely rare elements and very difficult to cultivate and nourish.

It is important to emphasize here the basic argument for supportive climates; that is, without them—with defensive climates—the flow of information is likely to become incomplete or distorted. Distorted information can cost money and make life unpleasant for managers and anyone else who needs accurate information.

Therefore, the intelligent creation of supportive climates is necessary. *Intelligent* is the key word. Supportive climates cannot be created the same way that a cake is baked or a building is constructed. A supportive climate cannot be "made" by mixing a dollop of "trust" with one-half pound of "participatory decision making." The human factors are too complex. If a manager tries to use a step-by-step cookbook approach and is careless and indifferent to the fragile nature of the human elements involved, the end result might not be an epicurean delight but a creation that could be toxic to the organizational system.

Cake dough is soft, malleable, and indifferent to manipulation. Employees are not. Any attempt to build supportive climates must be founded on the implicit recognition that the elements needed for supportive climates are multifaceted, variable, and even capricious—to the extent that humans are multifaceted, variable, and sometimes capricious. Nevertheless, managers can cultivate and create supportive climates.

This chapter is organized to discuss various aspects of this important component of the overall organizational communication program. It includes sections on:

- Supportive climates and teams
- Organizational credibility
- Motivating personnel
- Effective communication
- Goal articulation
- Interdependence of communication and climates
- Traditions and reputation
- Organizational tenacity
- The core factor
- A summary statement with caveats for managers

SUPPORTIVE CLIMATES AND TEAMS

Chris Ford was a starting guard for the 1981 world champion Boston Celtics. As professional basketball players go, he was not particularly skilled. He could not jump and he was not fast. He certainly could not dazzle you with any elements of his game. The only thing he could do, it seemed, was win. Chris Ford, in relatively intangible ways, was very capable of participating and contributing to the process of winning. While he certainly would have devoured the average schoolyard athlete in a game of one-on-one, he probably could not have competed with many other professional players in a similar individual contest. Yet he was a starter for the champions.

Over the years, the Boston Celtics (and other successful sports operations) have taken players who were cast-offs from other clubs and used them to enhance the quality of their overall operation. Celtic players Don Nelson and Dirk Minniefield come to mind. They had done little before coming to Boston but seemed to be willing to run in front of a freight train for the Celtics. Cedric Maxwell was brilliant for most of his career with Boston. He essentially became a nonentity once he was traded to the Los Angeles Clippers.

The Boston Celtics have won sixteen national basketball championships, and the reason this organization has been successful is not primarily because of superior individual talent and skills. The Celtics have won because their organization was a team. A team, not in any phony "we all love one another" sense, but a team in the sense of a group of people *committed to working together, in order to create an excellent product, for the purposes of realizing the group and individual rewards of success.*

The concept of *teams* in organizations is a controversial one. To many it smacks of ethereal, sixties, bohemian nonsense. The idea of cultivating a corporate culture meets with similar resistance. The British journal *Personnel Management* published an article in August 1984 titled, "Four Good Reasons Why When They Hear 'Culture' They Reach for the Aspirin."

Paul Buller and Cecil Bell, Jr. published an article in the *Academy of Management Journal* that summarized the research on teams and presented the results of their own study. Their research was inconclusive. Sometimes, they found, teams were effective, and sometimes they were not. The researchers essentially concluded that, "It is simply not clear why team building affects performance, if it does at all."

Yet the genuine commodity does affect performance. It is the ersatz variety that is not productive or counterproductive. Anyone who is or has ever been interested in team sports will acknowledge this. When a team is winning, the enthusiasm to work cooperatively to produce is contagious. When a team is losing, is poorly structured, has lazy players, or is managed by a megalomaniacal coach, the dissension that inevitably surfaces can devastate the team's chances. After baseball player Sid Gordon was traded to the hapless 1951 Pittsburgh Pirates, Gordon made the following observation.

"The trouble with these guys," he said, "is that after you've been with them for a couple of weeks you start to play like them."

There is nothing empty about the expression that in team sports the whole is greater than the sum of its parts. The same can be said for organizations and departments within organizations. If structured well, if composed of the right players, if the goals are clear and not spurious banalities designed to dupe the players to perform for the benefit of others, then the organization as a whole will perform more productively than it would if this team atmosphere were not present. And this more productive organization will permit and facilitate the accurate flow of information. The question is not whether teams can work, but how managers can create an atmosphere that is, indeed, a team atmosphere.

Supportive Climates, Teams, and Granfalloons

If you wish to study a granfalloon, just take the skin off a toy balloon.

So writes Kurt Vonnegut in his best-selling book, *Cat's Cradle*. A granfalloon, one of the many words Vonnegut has donated to the lexicon, is an organization with no substance—a body that appears to be meaningful, but after closer scrutiny is obviously meaningless.

One of the biggest problems with organizational teams and the creation of supportive climates is that these teams are often nothing more than granfalloons. Supportive climates that are granfalloons or are composed of granfalloons not only aren't substantive, but like the punctured balloon can make quite a pop when they are exposed.

No one wants to be part of a team that is really a bogus contrivance to get someone to work harder. No one wants to work together to create a corporate culture when that culture was fabricated as a ruse to dupe employees to sweat harder and longer to improve the lots of those who designed the "team."

Consider the following two examples.

Example 1: Troy and Spindler

     A recent college graduate, Troy, got her first job working for a small, fledgling, high-tech company. Her supervisor, Spindler, was also the chief executive officer of the tiny operation. Spindler told Troy that the company was new and because of the newness and the general attitude that people had at the company, she would be asked to work a week without pay. It was assumed, she was told, that new workers would put in a week gratis. In addition, she was informed that it was absolutely customary for her to work seven days a week. This, Spindler went on, was part of the corporate culture and team approach taken by the organization. On Sundays it would be fine, he said, if she took breaks now and then; work for a few hours, take a few hours off.

Because it was her first job, she went along with these requests, although she did so reluctantly. Soon she realized that the scenario Spindler portrayed was utterly false. She realized she'd been fooled to work a week for free (as had some others). She discovered that working Sunday was hardly normal for other employees. In short, she realized that the "team" he described was, without question, a granfalloon. When the skin came off the "toy balloon," she popped. Most of her hours at the job subsequently were spent in looking for other positions. Soon she got another job and left the "team."

Example 2: McCoy and Reynolds

David Reynolds, a low-level employee, was ready one Friday to leave town for the weekend. His supervisor, McCoy, approached him and told him that the organization needed him. What the organization/McCoy needed was for Reynolds to perform the most menial bit of labor that would have required that Reynolds work on Saturday without any additional compensation. Not aware of this extra chore until the moment that he was approached, Reynolds was nonplused when informed of these weekend responsibilities.

McCoy put his arm around Reynolds, gave a bit of a speech about this being a team effort, and then looked at Reynolds eyeball to eyeball. "David," he said solemnly. "This is your role on our team."

It would have been one thing if McCoy were being honest or if Reynolds indeed were needed to help with a genuine team effort. That simply was not the situation. McCoy needed some grunt work done, and figured he could finesse Reynolds into doing it.

Reynolds was a low-level employee, but he was not a fool. He realized that, very plainly, his manager did not want to do the work himself, and therefore, this suddenly was a grand team effort. Reynolds did not feel appropriately motivated. He felt that he was being duped and that the team was a charade. He was incensed.

Teams, not granfalloons, are part of the fabric of the supportive climate. Genuine team orientations, not "touchy-feely" artificial contrivances, can directly facilitate organizational productivity, efficiency, and effective communication. The development of a team attitude and the creation of supportive communication climates are fostered by the following organizational characteristics.

ORGANIZATIONAL CREDIBILITY

Management consultant and communication expert Roger D'Aprix conducted a study at a company where management had positioned huge billboards on the outside of the plant building. The billboards exhorted employees to strive for quality. When D'Aprix asked employees about the impact of the message, one burly guy looked at him and said with disgust, "Look, there are two signs you can believe around here. One says, 'wet paint;' the other says 'pardon our appearance.' The rest is baloney."

Organizational credibility is essential for the creation of supportive climates. It nourishes such climates. The absence of such credibility has a corrosive effect.

Under the heading of "No-No's" in *Up the Organization*, Robert Townsend makes the following suggestion regarding managerial credibility:

> "Except in poker, bridge, and similar play-period activities, don't *con* anybody.
>> Not your wife,
>> not your children,
>> not your employees,
>> not your customers,
>> not your stockholders,
>> not your boss,
>> not your associates,
>> not your suppliers,
>> not your regulatory authorities,
>> not even your competitors.
> Don't con yourself either."

Townsend was not real subtle. The next two examples comment on the problems that evolve from deception and a subsequent loss of credibility. The second example deals with individual credibility, yet the effects are applicable to organizations and managers with similar reputations.

Example 1:
    In January of 1977, Buffalo was buried under six feet of snow. While it takes some time to dig out from such a storm, the city's snow-removal effort seemed particularly slow, and many citizens complained. The mayor's office responded with something they called Operation Blitz.
    According to the spokespeople, Operation Blitz was going to be an unprecedented snow-removal effort. There would be plows working around the clock, and there would be nothing that would ambush the cleanup effort. The streets would be "blitzed" clean.

Through the media, the people of Buffalo heard a great deal about Operation Blitz. Despite the extensive municipal promises, the snow-removal effort continued to be inappropriately slow. Neighboring suburban communities with as much accumulation had clean streets and flowing traffic, while Buffalo was still buried days into the Blitz.

Local journalists began to investigate the matter and discovered that Operation Blitz bordered on being a sham. Operation Blitz appeared to be more an effort to placate a clamoring citizenry than an actual snow-removal effort. Journalists wrote of excessive overtime paid to sleeping "workers/blitzers," and there were reports of the use of inefficient and ineffective machinery.

Newscasters tried to investigate the extent of the actual cleanup. Reporters called citizens for reactions and street condition updates. In response to a journalist's query, one angry citizen allegedly barked, "They didn't 'blitz' here!"

The unrestrained assurances of Operation Blitz proved to be a credibility nightmare for the city. In retrospect, after having heard city officials declare the projected magnificence of Operation Blitz, Buffalo citizens would have done well to think of the Ralph Waldo Emerson line, "The louder he talked of his honor, the faster we counted our spoons."

Example 2:

A number of years ago I conducted a seminar in Western New York on improving presentation skills. Early in the seminar, a participant (Mitchell) gave a persuasive talk urging the other attendees to vacation in North Conway, New Hampshire and to avoid the more popular Florida jaunts.

The presentation was brilliant. He began by quoting others who had gone to North Conway, using these testimonials to enhance the attraction of a vacation at this New Hampshire retreat.

After referring to the testimonials, Mitchell displayed a map of the United States and illustrated in clear terms the difference in time, tolls—the toll on one's car and the toll on one's body—how much easier it would be to vacation in North Conway. Last, he produced a chart that indicated the costs for lodging and food in Florida as opposed to the relatively inexpensive costs in North Conway. Mr. Mitchell concluded emphatically that a trip to North Conway was, all things considered, an intelligent vacation choice.

As Mitchell sat down, I remarked that the speech was excellent and asked him when he had last been to North Conway.

"Ahhch," he shrugged. "I don't go there. Too many bugs."

At the time, the other seminar participants laughed heartily at this retort. Mitchell himself smiled at how he had amused the others. However, Mitchell was less than amused when he made his second presentation. This talk was about a serious topic, yet

Mitchell was unable to engage the audience into listening attentively. As far as the audience was concerned, he was "Too Many Bugs Mitch" and was not to be taken seriously.

Managers must resist taking misleading approaches to organizational problems. An Operation Blitz-type response may be enticing, but the damage to credibility lingers. Despite the fact that many people will say it is all right to lie in order to "get to yes," almost all people feel angry when they are misled. No one likes to be fooled, and if an organization is deceitful in its dealings with employees, the organization runs the great risk of developing a defensive climate in which employees are always "counting their spoons" when they receive information. After employees discover that management does not "go to North Conway" after all, they will be reluctant to pay serious attention to management's claims in the future. Simply, the climate and the overall organizational communication effort will be undermined if the organization's credibility is questionable.

The best and only advice is to be truthful and open, to the extent it is possible, with your organization or department. As Mark Twain once remarked, "When in doubt, tell the truth. You'll amaze some and astonish the rest."

MOTIVATING PERSONNEL

A high school football coach was asked to assess the team's chances for the upcoming season. The coach paused, sighed, and then said ingenuously, "We don't have the horses."

Managers need the horses also, not only to produce at maximum efficiency but also as a seed element of the supportive climate. The *horses* in organizations refer to a motivated population of workers, not just capable employees, but workers who will perform to their capacity. Motivating employees is complex. The section that follows discusses various factors that influence the creation of a motivated and capable workforce.

Recognizing Responsibilities and Purpose for Work

Employees must see and understand why it is important for them to do what they do. Employees who understand the purpose for expending energies and who see the bona fide fruit of such expenditures are likely to contribute to a supportive organizational climate. To illustrate this, consider the case of Richard Cook at the post office.

Richard Cook worked for the United States Post Office on the parcel post belt. The belt at this particular branch was a long conveyor type on which parcels that needed to be distributed to various communities traveled. Those who worked on the belt picked up individual parcels as they came by, read the addresses on the packages, and then tossed them into bins that were located on the opposite side of the belt from where Cook and his coworkers would stand.

The bins were alphabetically arranged so that towns like Babylon, Bay Shore, and Bethpage were located directly on the opposite side of the belt. However, the bins for Wyandich, Westbury, and Wantaugh were located several rows of bins away from the belt. Tossing parcels into the Amityville bin, for example, was easy. One had to be a sharpshooter to easily connect with the Valley Stream bin. To make matters worse, those who placed the parcels onto the belt actually did so by dumping entire sacks filled with parcels onto the belt at a rate of approximately three sacks a minute. In one quick dumping action, close to fifty parcels might come out of one sack.

Obviously, it would take much less time to dump fifty parcels than it would take to read the addresses on the parcels, aim, and throw the parcels into the correct bin. Invariably the belt would get overcrowded causing the parcels to crash into the end of the belt and then begin to rise and sometimes topple over into a Bethpage or Babylon container. To avoid this, Cook and others would often feverishly try to clear the belt, but in so doing would sometimes toss parcels indiscriminately just to get the belt cleared.

If the belt was so jammed that it could not be cleared no matter how feverishly the parcel post belt workers threw the packages, the manager would reluctantly turn off the conveyor until the belt could be cleared.

The dumpers considered it a victory of some strange sort when they would force the belt manager to shut down the conveyor. The belt manager did not like shutting down the conveyor, and would tell his employees to "Clear the belt, clear the belt!" in order to avoid such an eventuality.

The situation became more difficult on the day when the Record Club of America would mail their records. Literally hundreds of these flat parcels could be stuffed into one post office sack, and a dumper would wreak havoc by quickly dumping sacks filled with records onto the belt. Often, when the belt employees would have to deal with the records, they would toss them like Frisbees into any bin, capriciously, in a wild attempt to avoid having to shut down the conveyor.

On one day the postmaster was coming through the branch for an informal inspection and the branch managers were in a frenzy trying to look good . It was a Record Club of America day and the parcel post belt was stacked.

The belt manager became panicky and he continuously barked, "Clear the belt, clear the belt!" Finally Richard Cook stopped. Richard Cook pivoted around, stared at his manager, and simply said, "Why?"

It did not make any sense to keep throwing. There was not any logic to throwing the parcels into the wrong bin just to have them appear subsequently on the conveyor, again to be tossed, in all likelihood, into an incorrect bin.

Cook asked why, but the real question is how can managers motivate employees when these workers perceive their toil as foolishly meaningless. How can managers motivate employees when there is no answer to "Why?"

Managers have to make sure employees know why they are doing what they are doing. While it cannot be denied that some employees are not capable or desirous of doing much heavy thinking, the opportunity must be presented to them to allow them the chance, at least, to know what the purpose is for their work and how it fits into the "big" picture. The statement, "Just do it. Don't think. I'll do the thinking," is an all-too-often-heard comment. When employees cannot see the purpose for their work, they become disgruntled and may corrupt the organizational climate.

Screen Effectively

Groucho Marx once said, "I never forget a face, but in your case I'll make an exception." In order to have motivated personnel, managers need to effectively screen incoming employees and make intelligent exceptions.

This means screening employees not only in terms of what they can do but how they will interact with others. If managers make the intelligent assumption that such communication is vital, just as the actual physical constructing of a product is vital, then it is clear that an employee who is not willing or capable of interacting effectively with others is not a good person to let through the screen.

Nepotism and cronyism, of course, are toxic to the organizational system. If a supportive climate is the goal, then a motivated crew of employees is needed. The more dead wood that is in an organization, the tougher it will be to motivate the good people.

Find Strengths and Assign Responsibilities on the Basis of Strengths

Almost every person who gets through the screen has certain attributes that are areas of particular strength. A good policy is to assess what those attributes are and assign responsibilities on the basis of those strengths. It was a standard joke that the Army would take plumbers and make them medics, and take those with medical backgrounds and have them fix the pipes in the barracks. While it is important for employees to keep a broad outlook, it is essential that they are assigned to do whatever it is they excel at doing.

Delegate Responsibility

Managers who try to do everything are often not only not capable of doing one-half of what they set out to do but undermine the climate of the organization. Tacitly, if not outwardly, they are saying that they do not have confidence in the employees to do things for themselves. While there might be times when employees give managers good reason to question competence, as a general rule, managers must delegate responsibility to facilitate the creation of motivated personnel and a supportive climate.

A criticism frequently leveled at former President Jimmy Carter was that he was too engrossed in detail, and because of that, he eventually exhausted himself. I do not intimate here that President Carter's staff felt snubbed by this—in fact, President Carter's book *Keeping Faith*, Jody Powell's work *The Other Side of the Story*, and Hamilton Jordan's publication *Crisis* do not indicate that the Carter administration was beset by inner turmoil. I point this out only because Carter often did not delegate responsibility well and this may have tired him out.

As it relates to delegating responsibility and motivating personnel, the following example is valuable. The incident was controversial at the time (in sports' circles), and it dealt specifically with delegating responsibility in the form of participatory decision making.

> The Boston Celtics were preparing for the 1984 NBA final series with the Los Angeles Lakers, and the team was faced with the formidable problem of how to defend against Laker superstar Earvin "Magic" Johnson. Which one of the Celtic guards would play defense against Johnson?
>
> The coach of the Celtics, K.C. Jones, did not make the decision. He asked the two starting Celtic guards, Dennis Johnson and Gerald Henderson, which one wanted to "take" Magic Johnson. Gerald Henderson wanted the job and Dennis Johnson was amenable.
>
> Early in the seven-game series, Gerald Henderson had a very difficult time guarding Magic Johnson. To remain competitive, the Celtics were forced to switch defensive assignments on Magic Johnson and place Dennis Johnson on the Laker superstar.
>
> The press hounded K.C. Jones for allowing the players to make this crucial decision. "No coach asks players what to do," the press said. 'They tell them what to do."
>
> One writer approached Coach Jones and asked him directly, "How many coaches in the league do you think would have allowed their players to make such an important decision?"
>
> Jones replied simply, "I don't know, but can you tell me how many coaches are there participating in the finals?"

While the decision that the players made was not, in the final analysis, the wisest one, the climate that permitted them to make the decision may have been that which facilitated the Celtics' ultimate victory.

Delegating responsibility helps motivate employees. Of course, this delegation of authority does not require or invite the relinquishing of a manager's position at the "buck stops here" desk. Rather, it allows the employee to contribute and, therefore, improve morale. (See Chapter 3 for more information on this issue).

Assign Leaders and Not Megalomaniacs

Management is sometimes in the position to assign leaders. Sometimes these assignments take place when employees are hired or promoted. In any event, leaders ought to be those people who can and will lead, not people who see leadership as a place for exercising personal power. Also managers must lead by example. If a manager wants employees to be motivated they, in turn, must appear to be motivated.

Prepare for Nonmotivated Employees

Despite all precautions employees who cannot or will not be motivated will get through the screen. Managers should prepare for this eventuality and establish a fair system for purging them from the organization.

In short, motivated personnel are a key to a supportive climate. To get motivated personnel, managers need to be able to tell them why they should work hard and participate with this "team." Motivated personnel can be found by screening, finding strengths of individual workers, assigning responsibilities based on strengths, delegating responsibility, assigning/ hiring leaders, leading by example, and by preparing to deal with some incompetent, nonmotivated people in the organization.

If managers do not take the appropriate time when hiring and are sloppy when they assess an individual's strengths before assigning responsibilities, then they are going to pay the price down the road. And the price will directly and indirectly affect the quality of internal communication.

INTERDEPENDENCE OF COMMUNICATION AND CLIMATES

Since this entire book is based on the need for effective communication, it is unnecessary to dwell on the value of communication in this section. At this point, it suffices to write that effective communication is a necessary element for supportive climates, and supportive climates are likely to facilitate effective communication within the organization. That is, there is an interdependent relationship between climates and high-quality communication.

GOAL ARTICULATION

An organization is likely to be effective in creating a positive climate if it clearly expresses its goals and those goals are consistent with reality.

The aforementioned Roger D'Aprix comments that often top management feels that goals are clearly relayed when, in fact, they simply are not clearly relayed.

D'Aprix writes,

"When you talk to senior management they believe that objectives and issues of the business are fairly well understood.

They certainly can recite them with little hesitation. Yet as you interview people further down in the organization you find that there is less and less agreement and more and more confusion. And yet, how can people manage their own jobs if they don't understand the company priorities that should guide their work."

Consider the following example.

An organization hired Smith, a public relations person, to send out releases about a new product that the company was in the process of producing. After a week Smith realized that she was in trouble because of two enormous problems. The first problem was that the product had not been completed yet; therefore, she had difficulty knowing how to describe it. The second problem was that few engineers within the organization could agree on what the product would be like when it was finally completed. Nevertheless, the management wanted Smith to issue releases extolling the virtues of the product. The goal was to sell the product.

Not only was Smith issuing releases about a nonexistent product, but the company hired a fleet of salespersons to sell the product to consumers. When Smith mentioned her problem to management, she was sternly informed that the goals of the company were to sell this product and the company would not be deterred from its goals. If necessary, she was told, "Hose them down."

As any intelligent person could have predicted, the myopic policy of the company's management resulted in the near demise of the organization. Also the climate in the organization suffered because Smith, and others who were not deluding themselves, realized that they were in an untenable position. It was frustrating to work daily doing something that clearly did not make sense and would result, in the long run, in a tarnished reputation for the employee and the organization.

The clear articulation of organizational goals that make sense—and which facilitate the focusing of employee energy *on* those organizational and personal goals—will yield the type of supportive climate necessary for effective organizational communication and productivity.

When articulating goals, managers need not be excessively brash. A good rule is that if you have something powerful to say you do not have to say it powerfully.

I am reminded here of an incident that took place during a presentation skills seminar. At the beginning of the seminar each participant had to give a short introductory presentation. A newcomer (Johnson) approached me at the beginning of the second session and requested entry into the seminar. Johnson explained that he had not been able to attend the first session and would like to participate nevertheless. There was room for him in the group, and I told him it would be fine to enroll.

The way Johnson had spoken to me while requesting admission was in no way comparable to the manner of speaking he showed when introducing himself to the group. When speaking privately to me he had exhibited a soft, soothing speaking voice. He spoke quietly, not demonstratively. When he got in front of the others, he levelled a number of people sitting in the front row with a vocal blast that, somewhere, may have registered on the Richter scale. He bellowed his name, his future desires, and his present status with such volume that all those who were slouching rocketed to military posture from sheer fright.

I was stunned by his performance and attempted to maintain my equanimity to facilitate the conducting of the seminar. During a break, Johnson approached me. In his personal soothing tone he inquired, "How did I do? I want to improve my presentation skills so that I might move up in the organization. How was l?"

I immediately asked about the absence of such mellow tones when he was addressing the group.

"Aha," he replied. "You noticed." With a snicker, I noted that I had indeed noticed. He continued to explain.

"Well, you see, that's my plan—rock 'em, sock 'em, get 'em right in the gut."

I do not subscribe to the rock 'em-sock 'em school of speaking. Nor do I subscribe to the rock 'em-sock 'em school of most any communication diffusion. In articulating goals, managers must gain their employees' attention, clearly articulate, and guarantee receipt of the information as much as possible.

COMMITTED LEADERSHIP

The quality of the climate in the organization is likely to be enhanced if the leaders within the organization are willing to stand by the goals that they have set. Franklin Roosevelt reportedly said, "When you come to the end of your rope, tie a knot and hang on." Certainly, if the boat is going down quickly you must consider checking the maps, but if the leadership believes in the foundations upon which they have based the enterprise, then stay the course. Such perseverance to sensible goals is likely to facilitate supportive climates for the organization.

ESTABLISH INTELLIGENT ORGANIZATIONAL TRADITIONS AND MAINTAIN A REPUTATION AS A FAIR, CONCERNED EMPLOYER

Agreed, it is a mouthful. And as is the case with many other categories in this chapter, place this in the file marked "easier said than done." However, an organization that has a tradition of excellence and credibility has a relatively easy task when trying to create supportive climates.

Team building is simple when newcomers are greeted by veteran employees in much the same way as the Chamber of Commerce greets prospective merchants. When a coworker extols the virtues of the company on day one, it is easier for the rookie employee to believe and participate in a positive communication climate environment. Many companies enjoy excellent organizational climates because they have established a tradition of excellence which is passed on from veteran employees to newcomers.

RECOGNITION OF THE ESSENCE OF SUPPORTIVE CLIMATES

Recognizing that employees are human—with all the needs, desires, fallibilities, and energy of people—is at the core of supportive climates. When employees are managed as if they are chairs or inanimate cogs in a system, problems will inevitably arise. The Classical theory notwithstanding, people can be made to enjoy work.

Noel Coward wrote, "Work is much more fun than fun." It can be. American journalist Sydney Harris commented, "Few men ever drop dead from overwork, but many quietly curl up and die because of undersatisfaction." But perhaps psychiatrist Theodor Reik was most to the point when he said, "Work and love—these are the basics. Without them there is neurosis."

Managers who can genuinely tap employees' human needs and desire to do something fulfilling and rewarding with their lives will have taken a giant step toward creating the supportive climate that facilitates effective organizational communication.

SUMMARY

Supportive climates are one of the most important prerequisites for effective organizational communication. However, supportive climates have to be cultivated, much like land has to be cultivated. The necessary seeds for supportive climate cultivation include:

- Motivated personnel
- Organizational credibility
- Effective communication
- Organizational goal articulation
- Effective organizational leadership
- A genuine commitment to supportive climates
- Organizational traditions
- Recognition and respect for the human needs of employees

"Supportive" climates that are essentially bogus contrivances are only counterproductive. Supportive climates and corporate teams are often designed by people who have been told that teamwork and supportive climates are good for productivity. While this information is incontrovertibly accurate, the team should be designed by those who genuinely want supportive climates, not by employees interested in creating an ersatz team concept. If the supportive climate is clearly a contrivance, the end result can be devastating.

The organizational climate cannot be built by following a recipe. One absolutely needs "the horses" to have a supportive climate, and those horses must be able to not only "make the widget," but they also must be, if not personable, palatable.

It's difficult to ensure that an organization or even a department will be so populated. People come to work with assorted problems from their life experiences. It would be fine if everyone led idyllic existences and had peaceful childhoods, but few of us do. Without too much of a psychological digression, it's enough to write that employees come to the workplace with so many bags that it is difficult to create a supportive climate because the climate is simply burdened by the collected weight.

Supervisory personnel further complicate the problem of creating supportive climates. Managers cannot attempt to win "popularity contests," yet they must maintain good relations with their subordinates. These requirements are essentially in conflict, and therefore managers are forced to stay balanced on a narrow line.

Managers have both power and pressures. The power, for some, serves as an intoxicant. The pressures, for some, increase stress and decrease diplomacy. Individuals who become infused with an inflated sense of self-worth and who need the power of authority to allow them to function, can severely damage any efforts to create supportive climates in organizations. Individuals who are unable to deal with the stresses of supervision are likely to react to problems with poor communication skill, inevitably infecting the organizational climate.

In short, while supportive climates are crucial to managerial communication success, they are also very difficult to create and maintain. The heart of the organization (and the climate) is a function of the pedigree of the employees who work in the organization. Management, therefore, should do whatever it can to create a workforce of qualified, responsible, and personable individuals.

I suggest that interested readers refer to Appendix C which includes an article titled, "Turn the Beat Around: Meeting Human Communication Needs." This article deals with a particular case of contrasting managerial communication styles and the impact of these styles on productivity, motivation, and supportive climates.

5

Nonverbal Messages

An employee recently hired to work for the laconic Richard A. Wilson found himself seated next to Wilson during his first department meeting. At one point the employee offered a suggestion, and asked his boss what he thought of the idea. Wilson glanced at him and then looked across the table at his crony Jane Phillips. Phillips smiled. Wilson closed his eyes. He then opened them and slowly swiveled his head away from Phillips in order to return to the employee. Wilson spoke softly and said, "It's fine." Then he paused, and wrote a note to himself. Wilson finished his note and looked up at the employee again with an enigmatic smile.

> Abraham Lincoln once remarked, "[It's] better to remain silent and be thought a fool than to speak out and remove all doubt."

Lincoln's remark was probably intended to discourage people from speaking thoughtlessly. In some cases his advice is most wise. However, it is important to know and note that being silent does not preclude the perception of meaning. Silence may not definitively convey intelligence or ignorance, but it may well convey something to a particular receiver. That is, most receivers attempt to "read" the nonverbal dimensions of a message and, therefore, do perceive meaning—accurately or otherwise—from silence or other nonverbal behaviors.

In fact, in organizations and elsewhere, *most of what receivers perceive is based on nonverbal information.* According to researcher Albert Mehrabian, ninety-three percent of that which is communicated is a function of nonverbal factors and only seven percent is based on verbal information. Some researchers quibble with the figure Mehrabian uses. Some claim that sixty-five percent is based on nonverbal messages. Others argue the percentage is in the eighty percent range.

Whatever statistic you believe, clearly nonverbal messages are important factors affecting communication success. Managers who are concerned with their communication must understand the significant role nonverbal messages have in the sending and receiving of organizational information.

MYTHS AND MISCONCEPTIONS

Body Language and Nonverbal Messages

At a presentation skills seminar I conducted recently, a speaker named Brandon made a presentation about insurance options. Brandon, I noticed, was punching a fist into the air intermittently throughout the speech. The action looked a bit like a jab, as if Brandon was preparing for an upcoming bout with a heavyweight. I tried to see if there was any correlation between his jabs and what he was saying at the time of the punch. There was none.

At the end of the seminar, I asked him about the unusual gesturing. Brandon smiled and told me that he was throwing some body language into the speech for effect.

There are many misconceptions about nonverbal messages and body language. Certainly as it relates to Brandon, a myth that needs to be purged is that aimless "body language" has a positive effect. Throwing some body language into a communicative effort for the sake of reaching a certain quota is nonsense.

Another misconception regarding this subject is that the phrase "body language" is synonymous with nonverbal communication. The phrases are not synonymous. What is loosely referred to as body language is only an aspect of nonverbal message study. While it certainly is an important aspect, it is only a facet of those nonverbal factors that affect the perception of messages.

In general, the term *body language* is used incorrectly most of the time. Part of the incorrect usage is related to the second myth about nonverbal messages.

The Relationship of Nonverbal Acts to Specific Units of Meaning

A woman who I work with had an apartment that she wanted to rent. The woman, Alton, approached me about the apartment as she knew that I was looking for a new place. I visited Alton's flat and then told her that I needed some time to make a decision. She said she would hold the place for me for a week as long as I was seriously considering it.

The next day I happened to bump into Alton in the hallway while I was hurrying to meet a class for which I was late. She waved a "hello" and stopped in the hallway. I hesitated momentarily, but knew that I had to keep moving in order to avoid being even more tardy. I smiled, said, "Gotta run," on the move, and continued to my class.

Two days later I decided to rent Alton's apartment and phoned her. When I told her of my decision, she expressed surprise and informed me that the place had been rented. I was stunned, and I reminded her that she had said she would hold it for me for a week.

At this point, Alton said that she had deduced from our encounter in the hallway that I was no longer interested in the apartment. She told me that she could tell by the way I reacted to our coincidental meeting that I was not really interested in the place since I had avoided the subject when we had met. I quickly responded that I had not avoided any subject but had been in a hurry to make a class.

"Oh," she said. "I thought you didn't want the place. I'm sorry."

This example illustrates the second misconception about nonverbal messages—i.e., one that is promulgated particularly by those who refer to all nonverbal messages as body language. That myth is that there is always a one-to-one relationship between a nonverbal act and specific units of meaning.

As discussed in Chapter 1, communication is a receiver-oriented phenomenon—i.e., what is communicated is that which is received by a receiver. Crossing arms, for example, does not mean anything in and of itself. Different receivers will glean different meanings from that act. Speaker pacing does not necessarily mean anything, although many receivers might think that a speaker who paces is nervous. Motions, expressions, and intonations may be perceived as meaningful, but they (usually) do not "mean" the same thing to all receivers.

This myth of a one-to-one relationship is spread frequently. Consider the following statements excerpted from a widely-read magazine.

Open hands and an unbuttoned coat indicate an openness about a person.

Suspicion is indicated by crossed arms, glancing sideways, touching or rubbing the nose or the eyes, buttoning the coat, and drawing away.

Cooperation is shown with open hands, sitting on the edge of the chair, unbuttoning the coat, tilting the head, and hand to face gestures.

Body movements that indicate reflection include peering over one's glasses, taking one's glasses off or cleaning them, pipe smoking gestures, biting on the end of one's glasses, and putting one's hand on the bridge of the nose.

This information is simply false. Open hands might indicate cooperation to some people. To others it might indicate something else, if it indicates anything at all to them.

Those who make claims that certain actions *mean* certain things to all people are making erroneous claims. There *are* specific nonverbal actions that have one-to-one relationships between the action and a unit of meaning. They are called *emblems* and will be discussed shortly. By and large, however, nonverbal actions are perceived differently by different receivers. They, absolutely and unequivocally, are perceived—there's no argument about that—but interpretations of nonverbal messages vary greatly.

If a person folds his hands in front of his stomach, he might be uptight; he might have been fat as a kid and is somehow trying to hide what he perceives to be an unattractive midriff bulge; or he might have an obscene tattoo on his wrist and is covering one hand with the other to conceal an unclad lady. The act, in and of itself, is not part of a secret "body language." There could be multiple perceptions of the act.

Nonverbal messages often contribute to communication problems in organizations because they:

- Play such a large part in employee perceptions
- *Do not have universal meanings*
- Are often inaccurately decoded

If nonverbal messages did have universal meanings, it would be significantly easier to communicate effectively.

If I were to ask, "Where is Marco?" almost any person would know that I was looking for Marco. But if I were saying little at a conference table, the meeting participants might think that I disagreed with the proposals on the table, that I was uninterested, *or any of a variety of other things*. And all of those different things that were perceived would be that which had been communicated to the individuals who made those perceptions.

Nonverbally, I had communicated to my colleague, Alton, that I did not want her flat. Certainly, I did not want to send that information to her, but that was the message that she received. Often in organizations, information we do not want to communicate is communicated whether we like it or not. Frequently, given the large play it has in the communication setting, the problem is rooted in a nonverbal factor that has influenced the receipt of information.

CATEGORIES OF NONVERBAL MESSAGES

The focus in this section is on defining each of nine nonverbal message categories and then illustrating how each factor can affect managerial behavior.

Paralanguage

Paralanguage refers to how we say what we say, and it is an extremely important nonverbal message category. It is a good example of a type of nonverbal communication that has little to do with body motion or size.

Paralanguage refers to nonverbal vocal factors, including rate of speech, voice tone, volume, emphases, accents, rhythm of speech, and nonverbal interjections. These factors affect the perception of messages. Sometimes this nonverbal category is called *vocalics*. (A common misuse of the words *verbal* or *verbalize* is to equate these words with the terms *vocal* or *vocalize*. To *verbalize* simply means to put into words, which can be done orally or in writing). Unfortunately, the content of a message is sometimes less important than the vocalic factors that surround that content.

I remember listening to two speakers on consecutive days while attending a management communication seminar in Western New York. The speakers represented different corporations in the Buffalo area who were explaining the nature of their respective organizations' operations to the participants in the seminar.

On the first day, Glick spoke. He came prepared. His presentation was organized and filled with information. However, his paralingual speaking qualities were awful. Glick sounded like he did not want to be there. His volume was inadequate. The rhythm of his speech was predictable. Words that were emphasized were emphasized only slightly, and even in these cases, it seemed like the decision to emphasize one word over another was arbitrary.

The second day Brenner spoke to our group. Brenner was as smooth an orator, vocally, as one could want to hear. He varied his rate of speech, emphasized words appropriately, spoke with enough volume to be heard without speaking too loudly and, in short, held the attention of the participants simply by expertly dealing with vocalic factors.

Unfortunately, Brenner had absolutely nothing of substance to say. I paid particular attention to the content of the presentations, and knew that between Glick and Brenner there was no comparison in terms of substance. Indeed, there was no comparison in terms of the paralingual style of the presentation either.

At the conclusion of the seminar the speakers were evaluated. Glick was panned like a bad movie. Brenner was extolled and many in the group wanted to reach him to see if he would be willing to speak to their particular groups.

For better or worse, the Glick and Brenner incident is not at all unusual. Paralingual factors are often more important than the verbal factors in communication because paralingual factors are typically perceived to be more believable.

Assume that you asked a new employee how things were going and s/he responded, "Just great." Let's say "just great" didn't sound just great. What would you believe—the nonverbal vocal message that you thought you "heard" or the meaning of the words themselves? Most people tend to believe the vocal message and not the verbal message. Certainly one has the option of repeating the question or rephrasing it to be certain that one's "read" of the response is accurate. Sometimes, however, people are reluctant to do so. In some contexts (conferences, for example), you might not be able to ask a follow-up question.

In subtle yet potentially damaging ways, the overriding paralingual factors can affect the nature of managerial communication and managerial relationships with subordinates. Consider the following comments from an unhappy employee.

> The worst communication problem I had in an organization occurred in my previous job. The problem was between my supervisor and me. This woman constantly, from day one, spoke to me in a very patronizing and condescending way that I could not tolerate. Every time I would approach her to speak with her, she would respond in her usual manner, which each time aggravated me more and more. This woman was communicating with me in the same manner as she would speak to her daughter, who is 16.
>
> Because of her lack of communication skills in dealing with me, she was making the situation worse and worse until it came to a point where I could no longer speak with her, because I would get too upset. This problem eventually led to my quitting the job.
>
> Had she been more aware of how her manner of communicating with me was affecting my attitude, and if she could have improved her skills, perhaps it would not have led to my quitting.

Often people have paralingual problems and are not even aware of it. The supervisor in this situation may not have known that her manner was exasperating. The employee would have been wise to confront the supervisor, but not all employees are so inclined or courageous. The end result is the loss of an employee for reasons related to nothing more than an infuriating paralingual communication style.

Another extremely important aspect of paralanguage relates to the inclusion of interjections in communication. Almost without exception, whenever I ask a group what is the single most annoying factor to them as listeners, they say it is the use of "ers," "ahs," "ums," and "you knows."

In the case of a former client, it was as if the word, "okay," had taken the place of a period. In describing a problem in his organization he would typically say:

Let me tell you what happened at the meeting yesterday. Okay. I got to the meeting five minutes ahead of time, okay. When I got there, I was the only person there or so I thought, okay. So, I sat down with my coffee at the table, okay, and I hear James, okay, talking to Harriet, okay, about how they're going to make sure that the topic of pension increases never comes up at the meeting, okay. Now, you tell me, okay, is that a hidden agenda or what, okay?

A high school math instructor used to use the interjection "a-umm" so often in the course of his lectures that the students stopped listening to his instructions and began counting the "a-umms." This reaction is not that uncommon. Often, when a communicator pervades messages with interjections, the receivers will focus on the frequency of the interjections as opposed to the content of the message.

Typically speakers are unaware of the frequency of their interjections. At one point, I informed my "okay" client of his habit and he was stunned. It took him only a short time to reduce the "okays" in his speaking repertoire.

Paralanguage can make a dolt seem intelligent, and paralanguage can make a brilliant employee seem relatively valueless.

Physical Characteristics

A number of years ago I found myself waiting at night at a Los Angeles bus stop. I was in a seedy, unfamiliar area, and I became increasingly uncomfortable as I waited for the bus. Drunks stumbled out of bars, unsavory characters lurked on street corners, and a scuffle broke out in a nearby alley. I did not feel particularly safe and could not wait much longer for the bus to arrive.

Moments after the streetfight had abated, a six-foot, four-inch, 240-pound bruiser carrying an attaché case joined me at the bus stop. My large comrade was dressed in a handsome vested suit, and despite the late hour, was wearing sunglasses. I planned to stay with him. No one, I figured, would battle with that physical specimen, so I decided that no matter where this man went, I would follow.

My companion moved to the left. I took a few steps to the left. He moved to the right, and I followed suit as if I were his shadow. After a while of this "Simon Says" routine, my companion looked to the left, quickly looked to the right, and then glanced down at me.

"I don't know about you fellah, but I'm scared. I'm getting out of here."

With that, my "savior" raced up the block dragging his attaché case. I took off after him like an Olympic sprinter. When I caught him, he wheezed, "That's a dangerous area, man. Let's run up the block this-a-way and catch the bus up the line where it's safer. Two people were murdered down here last week, man. Let's move."

The point here is that on the basis of the physical qualities of my large acquaintance I assumed that he was fearless and that I was safe by his side. This perception was inaccurate, as I discovered when he darted away. Often, people inaccurately perceive information on the basis of someone's physical appearance. Physical factors such as height, weight, attractiveness, and complexion affect that which is received by receivers.

An enormous man, nicknamed Tiny by his friends, was attending a seminar which I conducted for emergency medical technicians. One night after class, Tiny gave me a ride home. During the ride, he explained that being large can present severe problems. For example, he told me that he never goes into bars, because nine times out of ten, some drunken lout will approach him wanting to fight. Tiny went on to explain that usually these tavern dwellers would get some liquid courage into their systems and say to him, "You think you're tough. You're not so tough." Tiny said that if he answered honestly, he would say, "I know I'm not so tough."

When prospective employees enter the interview setting, they are often assessed on the basis of how they dress (a nonverbal category that will be discussed shortly) and what they look like.

The anecdotes about the Los Angeles bus stop and Tiny illustrate that physical factors will be perceived regardless of whether they are correct or incorrect. It is essential, therefore, that communicators recognize the reality of physical factors in the communication process.

Chronemics

A client once commented that her manager was a considerate, responsible, and efficient supervisor. Her basis for this conclusion was that the manager was almost always on time when she had appointments with her and because of this punctuality the client had concluded that the manager was responsible, consistent, and efficient.

She may be incorrect in this deduction. Certainly, if she was to generalize that the manager was always responsible, considerate, and efficient in her nonprofessional interactions, she might be incorrect. Nevertheless, she had this reaction to the manager.

Similarly, on the basis of how time affects communication, termed *chronemics,* receivers perceive various types of information. For example, information is perceived when individuals are habitually late to meetings, are unusually garrulous and time-consuming on the phone, take repeated telephone calls when in a conference, and deliver presentations that go over the allotted time.

If an employee submitted a request for a leave of absence and did not hear anything on the request for a month, that employee might assume that the request would not be granted. The employee might figure that the grapevine would have carried the positive information if s/he were getting the leave. The nonverbal factor of time would have been perceived by the employee to be meaningful. Of course, s/he might be incorrect.

It is important to note, as potential senders of information, that time is often perceived as having meaning. As receivers, it is important to recognize that we all make assumptions on the basis of time and often do so inaccurately.

Touch

Haptics refers to the study of touch and how touch communicates. According to traditional business practices, prospective candidates were told to greet potential employers with a firm handshake. This firm handshake was supposed to convey information. Firm handshakes do convey information, perhaps differently to different audiences. The basis of haptic study is the reality that handshakes and other touching behavior are perceived as meaningful.

Unless a person is a fledgling Leo Buscaglia and hugs audience members while making presentations, the influence of touching is likely to affect the interpersonal communication context as opposed to other organizational communication contexts. In the interpersonal context, touching behavior is very important, as it is subject to considerable misinterpretation and, therefore, often negatively affects the accurate receipt of information. The following example illustrates this point.

> A colleague commented that as a youngster he found that one side of his family was a very "huggy" bunch. He claimed that as soon as he entered someone's home for a family gathering, he would be attacked by distant aunts that he did not even recognize. The other side of his family was much more restrained. He was greeted warmly when he visited with them, but there was a definite absence of hugging. As a youngster, my colleague made the incorrect assumption that one side of the family cared more for him than the other.

People in organizations also make assumptions on the basis of touching behavior; these assumptions are often incorrect. A supervisor might place a hand on the shoulder of a subordinate when relaying news. Employees might embrace one another when saying good-bye for a vacation. Workers might even hold hands when preparing for some cooperative effort. One of the more incongruous examples of employee hand-holding was evident each time the defensive unit of the 1973 Denver Broncos huddled before a play. Before each snap of the ball the defenders would huddle and hold a teammate's hand before they would break to assume their defending positions.

Nevertheless, information is perceived on the basis of touch. People do interpret touching behavior and take with them some meaning, accurate or otherwise, from that touching behavior.

Kinesics

Kinesics refers to the study of body movement, and how it conveys meaning. Kinesic behaviors include gesticulations, facial expressions, running, speed of walking, and any body movement that may be perceived by someone as either meaningful, in and of itself, or that which complements other verbal and nonverbal messages.

One category of kinesic behavior is called *emblems*. Emblems can be defined as motions that have a one-to-one relationship between that motion and a certain unit of meaning. Consider the situation in which a motorist is attempting to parallel park and is being assisted by a good samaritan pedestrian. The pedestrian waves the motorist back indicating how much space the driver has before the automobiles collide. This action is emblematic because, given the context and culture, that gesture has as specific a meaning as the most concretely defined word.

It is important to note that emblems are *context* and *culture* bound. Consider the following excerpt from the *Vietnam Photo Book:*

> Count certain generals in the ten percent that normally fail to get the word. Some apparently haven't caught on to the fact that the World War II Churchill "V for victory" sign is being used by anti-war groups as a peace symbol. In one news report quoting the two-star general involved, the post commander admitted he had been exchanging the peace sign with soldiers for three months before learning its current meaning.

Some kinesic behaviors are not emblems but are *illustrators*, which in and of themselves carry no specific meaning, but when complemented with certain utterances, become close to emblematic. For example, assume that I am telling a subordinate that it is essential for him to be on time for future meetings:

> "Now *look*, Jones, you are *just* going to *have* to *make* an effort to get *here* on *time*."

Assume that paralingually I emphasize the words "look," "just," "have," "make," "here," and "time." If while I emphasize these words, I simultaneously point a finger at Jones, the kinesic behavior—the pointing—becomes essentially emblematic. This type of complementary kinesic behavior is called an *illustrator.* By itself, the gesture is like any other type of nonverbal message in that it is subject to varied perceptions. But when complemented by a consistent verbal utterance, it takes on emblematic meaning.

Some kinesic behaviors are emblematic because of certain learned characteristics of the culture. Anyone who has ever been a student knows how to assume a pose that implies that the student is paying attention. When someone asks a particularly difficult question, we might find ourselves scratching our head with a finger or two, implying that we are thinking about it, as if such scratching might activate dormant gray matter. Often people will look skyward when ostensibly involved in deep thought, as if perhaps the answer could be found by consulting some celestial force. These kinesic behaviors are essentially learned emblems.

(There is a clear distinction between these behaviors and those referred to earlier—open hands indicating cooperation, buttoning the coat indicating suspicion, etc. The motions listed in the previous paragraph are arguably emblematic. Even so, they too can be subject to some varied interpretations.)

There are many kinesic behaviors, however, that are not emblematic nor are they illustrators. Sometimes people have individual kinesic manner-isms that are enigmatic to all but those who know these individuals well. What appears as nervous hand-twitching to many might be a habit that a person has never broken. It could have many actual meanings, but a receiver could infer other, unintended, meanings as well.

A speaker that I listened to recently waved his arms so wildly during his presentation that he appeared ready to take off. To many he appeared to be "spacey" because of these indecipherable gesticulations.

A former colleague furrowed his brow into an ominous-looking scowl while contemplating serious problems. Most newcomers assumed that J.B. was furious ninety percent of the time because of this facial expression. The fact was that J.B. was often dealing with serious problems. His facial contortions were simply his own.

Almost all of us have experienced being asked "What's wrong?" when nothing is really wrong. Almost all of us have asked others "What's wrong" on the basis of the others' expressions. Sometimes these questioners have perceived the kinesic behavior accurately and there has been effective communication. Sometimes there is indeed nothing wrong. Receivers have just incorrectly perceived the facial expression.

Olfactics

Olfactics is the study of smell and how messages are perceived by the olfactory system. Unless an individual is particularly ripe, olfactics will not affect presentation settings. Olfactics can and does affect interpersonal communication and conference communication.

Olfactics is a sensitive area of communicative behavior. It is very difficult to tell subordinates, peers, and particularly supervisors that they are offensive. One might be inclined to tell others that they speak too loudly, or that they use too many "you knows" while conversing. However, even lovers and family members have trouble discussing bad breath or other annoying body odors. It has been surprising to me to discover how often employees cite olfactics as a problem in their organizational communica-tions. The following case is not too dissimilar from many others that I have heard.

Sharon Singer manages a small, one-floor, nine-employee department. An extremely efficient employee, Wilke, worked in an enclosed cubicle and dealt with financial matters related to the company. As long as she remained in that cubicle there were no problems. However, occasionally she would emerge to discuss financial issues with various members of the company.

Whenever Wilke would come out of her cubicle, she brought with her an unpleasant odor that would literally stop work. Singer eventually confronted Wilke on the issue. She informed Wilke that other employees had complained. The others did not want to work with such an unclean coworker. Wilke explained that she was on medication that had, as a side effect, this terribly offensive odor. There was some doubt as to the authenticity of Wilke's explanation, as some research on the alleged medication indicated that its side effects need not have been so extreme.

Despite the confrontation, the problem did not get better. It became a standard "joke" of sorts. Eventually, Singer was forced to let Wilke go, despite her efficiency with numbers.

Not all olfactic communication deals with employees emitting unpleasant odors. However, the reality of smell affecting that which is perceived is incontrovertible. The success of the cologne industry supports this. People are aware on some conscious or subconscious level that the way one smells affects how others perceive them. That is, they recognize that smell conveys information to receivers.

Proxemics

Proxemics is the study of space and how space affects the communication process. It is a very important nonverbal aspect of organizational communication.

A good place to notice the effect that space has on communication is in an elevator. Typically, when people walk into an elevator they walk to the back of the space, place their backs to the far wall, and turn to face the door of the elevator. At that time riders often look up at the floor numbers and continue to focus on those numbers during the ride. Interpersonal interactions might take place in elevators, but both people still usually face the door while gazing at the illuminated floor numbers. That same conversation taking place outside the elevator would have the participants facing one another.

Simply, space affects the nature of interactions and communicates varied messages to receivers. People with large offices, for example, might be perceived as having more authority than those with less space. People on the top floor of a building might be seen as, and indeed might be, more powerful. In public speaking scenarios the spatial configuration of the audience has an effect on the success of the speaker. For this reason, speakers often ask participants to move down to the front or to sit in certain configurations. In conferences, the arrangement of the participants is often meant to reflect the power of the individual participants.

The silliest, albeit illustrative, example of this took place during the Paris Peace Talks, held during the Vietnam War. Before the talks could begin, angry participants refused to convene because of the shape of the conference table. Certain members wanted to sit in certain specific places. The peace talks were stalled because the peacemakers could not agree on the spatial relationship that would exist between the mediators. It was easy to become skeptical about the potential for success of this peace conference.

Often, proxemic factors (as is the case in certain haptic scenarios as well) are a function of culture and custom. In interpersonal communication, people typically require their own personal space. They can become aggravated if their receivers encroach on their personal space. Sometimes people encroach on personal space to try to intensify a point, or because others are unaware of the messages that are being perceived by those whose space is being taken.

The physical spatial design of an organization, the space between others in interpersonal and conference communication, and the space that separates people in presentational contexts can all be perceived as meaningful, and, therefore, should be considered by those who communicate in organizations.

Artifacts

Artifacts are those things made by humans. Archaeologists, of course, typically look for artifacts, hoping to find some clues as to the nature of earlier civilizations. In the analysis of nonverbal messages, artifacts refer to things, made by humans, which convey meanings to receivers. Dress and jewelry are two common factors that fall into the category of artifacts.

For better and mostly for worse, people are often evaluated on the basis of things that they wear. The expression, "clothes make the man," is sadly too often on the mark. An old salesperson's wheeze is that one should always polish the back of one's shoes, because that's the last thing a buyer sees.

It is certainly true that receivers perceive a great deal of information on the basis of how others are dressed. Undeniably, behavioral assessments are made on the basis of clothing. For this reason, people take great care—as they should, given the great impact it has on message perception—in how they are dressed.

Prospective employees consider what they will wear to an interview. Speakers debate about the appropriate attire for a presentation. Organizations evaluate the wisdom of imposing dress codes on employees. If artifacts did not affect message perception, these types of deliberations would be unnecessary. Speakers must continue to be concerned with dress, and receivers must work hard not to let artifacts affect perceptions of others to too large an extent.

Very recently an applicant, Elliot, was rejected for a job at ITD Corporation. Elliot, an extremely competent professional, had come to the interview dressed informally. In speaking with him subsequently, Elliot told me that he had guessed wrong about the nature of the organization. He had thought that the organization wanted a less than stuffy look for the employees. Elliot is not the sort of person who would balk at the requirement of a dress code. He is a company type—a "team" player. Nevertheless, he was rejected for the job. The interviewer, without confronting the issue directly, assumed that Elliot would not fit in because he chose to dress informally for the interview. Elliot was out of a job, and ITD was out of a high-quality performer because of inaccurate perceptions of nonverbal messages.

Oculesics

The final category for analysis is eye contact, termed *oculesics*, and how it affects communication. In interpersonal, public, and conference communication contexts, oculesics is an extremely important factor affecting the receipt of messages.

Think about the last excellent presentation you heard. Imagine that presentation a bit differently. Imagine what it would have been like had the speaker delivered the presentation while looking above the heads of the collective audience during the entire presentation. Obviously, the eloquence of the speaker would have been lost if that was the nature of the speaker's eye contact.

In public speaking scenarios, speakers have to exhibit frequent and sustained eye contact to facilitate the receipt of information. If receivers do not get frequent and sustained eye contact, they will likely perceive a variety of information that distracts them from the intended message.

In interpersonal communication contexts, it is most annoying when the person with whom you are talking will not look at you. The reasons for this absence of eye contact might vary. It could be due to nervousness, because the sender is conveying bad news, or because of some factor related to the individual history of the person speaking. Nevertheless, the absence of eye contact will have an effect.

Similarly, excessive eye contact might be perceived as having more meaning than the source intends. There are people who seem to be trying to "gaze a hole" through another when talking about what appears to be rather mundane issues. The receiver may likely begin to wonder about the meaning of the heavy eye contact and make determinations, often incorrect, about the unusual gazing.

During conferences, participants who are not speaking at any one time may pan other attendees to attempt to assess the reaction that the others have to the positions being stated. What group members do with their eyes often have a variety of meanings, often as many meanings as there are participants in the conference.

Speakers who do not utilize their eye contact effectively are destined to have difficulty. Simply, a presenter's audience will likely perceive distracting meanings from inadequate eye contact.

Receivers must be careful not to be wowed by those *who are able* to maintain a steely gaze in interpersonal, conference, or presentation contexts. The ability to maintain strong, but not overbearing, eye contact is atypical, and it is often perceived as a character strength. While it might be, it also might be a simple communicative skill that the sender might have which reflects only sound coaching.

SUMMARY

A large percentage of what is perceived is dependent on nonverbal factors. Managers must recognize the nature and possible impact of nonverbal messages on the perception of information. Eye contact, paralanguage, and spatial relationships, for prime examples, can play a significant role in determining the quality of communication.

6

Improving
Presentations

In July 1987 Lieutenant Colonel Oliver North wowed the American public, and within the course of one short week went from potential villain to national hero. Crowds shouted hosannas for North, chanting "OL-LEE, OL-LEE," the same way that boxing enthusiasts used to cheer for former heavyweight champion Muhammud Ali. People sent North thousands of telegrams wishing him support, and the Lieutenant Colonel found himself on the cover of almost every major news magazine in the country.

The primary reason for North's instant success was nothing other than North's excellent communication skills. Oliver North was a brilliant speaker. He was eloquent. He was forceful vocally. He was expressive with gesturing and eye contact. He wowed the television viewing public because of his ability to speak publicly in a way few others can.

Our history is marked by leaders who had, as an unusual skill, an ability to speak well. Ronald Reagan, aptly dubbed the great communicator, had an innate ability to speak in front of crowds. This ability played no small part in his so-called "Teflon" presidency. John Kennedy and Martin Luther King are two other politicians who were successful in large part because of their excellent speaking skills. On the downside of this phenomenon, there is the specter of the eloquent Adolph Hitler mobilizing the masses in Germany to participate in atrocities so incredible that even the incontrovertible evidence leaves honorable people incredulous.

The power of public speaking is, simply, one of the strongest weapons humans have. As existential philosopher Jean Paul Sartre commented, "Words are loaded bullets."

To a lesser extent in terms of international ramifications, organizational communicators can make careers out of excellent presentation skills or can be ruined because of their fears of speaking in front of people. In a sense, what separates great business leaders from the average ones is not their great ideas but their capacities to express these ideas and convey them to others.

This chapter will deal with the issues of presentations in organizations, including:

- Presentation styles
- Structuring content
- Questions and answers
- Persuasive messages
- Stage fright

PRESENTATION STYLES

All presentations can be grouped into one of four styles. Speeches are either impromptu, extemporaneous, manuscript, or memorized presentations.

Impromptu presentations are "off-the-cuff" presentations that are delivered without any preparation. Responses to questions, when the inquiry was not anticipated, also fall into the category of impromptu speeches.

Extemporaneous presentations are those that are delivered from notes. The notes can be as detailed as a formal outline or as brief as a few words listed on a 3-by-5 index card. Many, if not most, corporate presentations fall into this category. Even when speakers are following an outline that is memorized (note that the outline is memorized; not each word in the presentation) the presentation is said to be extemporaneous. In extemporaneous talks, speakers use the outline to spark recollections of the message to be conveyed, but must, while in front of the audience, select the correct word to match the ideas.

Manuscript presentations are delivered, *not read*, from a prepared text. Many formal business presentations are essentially manuscript speeches and these can be appropriate depending upon the occasion and the experience of the speaker.

Memorized presentations are simply manuscript speeches that have been committed to memory. A presentation is only classified as a memorized speech if the delivery is a word-for-word memorization.

Using Different Styles: Advantages and Disadvantages

During any communication, the goal is to reach the receiver with the intended message, and public presentations are no exception. However, in public communication, as opposed to other types of communication—

interpersonal or group, for example—the speaker has a distinct and important advantage. A speaker can plan out the best possible method for facilitating the accurate receipt of the message. The speaker can analyze the nature of the audience, the nature of the situation, and the nuances of the room within which the speech will be given. In short, the speaker can and should prepare comprehensively in order to maximize the chances for effective receipt of information.

Impromptu Formats

There are very few advantages to using impromptu formats when making presentations. When speakers use impromptu formats they are essentially "blowing" the advantage that public communication contexts afford. The simple reason why we hear so many impromptu speeches despite the dubious wisdom of such a choice is because many people prefer not to invest the energy necessary to prepare for the other presentation formats. They prefer to be lazy and "wing it."

It is good for speakers *to be able to* make impromptu talks, however. There are times when people simply have to deliver speeches in this way. If at a large meeting, for example, the coordinator suddenly calls on a participant and says, "Why don't you come on up here and tell us what you've been doing over these past few months." The participant's ensuing description of activities will be an impromptu presentation.

Additionally, as briefly mentioned earlier, if at the end of an extemporaneous or manuscript speech, the speaker solicits questions from the audience, the answers to these questions will be impromptu speeches. Such rejoinders would not be impromptu speeches if the speaker had anticipated the questions and had prepared responses for the anticipated queries.

During the Contra hearings, Oliver North and his attorney Brendan Sullivan were brilliant in this regard. North demonstrated throughout the hearings that he is an excellent impromptu speaker. However, for many of the congressmen's questions, North was ready with an extemporaneous response as he and his attorney had speculated on what questions might likely surface during the inquiry.

In short, the impromptu style is the lazy person's approach. While some speakers might be able to wow folks with their verbal dexterity when employing this format, the speaker is more likely to negatively impress the audience. Only when no other alternative is possible should the impromptu presentation style be selected.

Memorized Formats

Memorized formats are also problematic, and are strongly discouraged. Unless one is an actor or actress, memorized speeches pose many more disadvantages than advantages. Remember, a memorized speech is a manuscript speech committed to memory. Actors and actresses spend months trying to get scripts "right." Most speakers do not have months to get their manuscripts right. Trying to memorize the manuscripts in their entirety, and subsequently delivering the speeches in this memorized mode, can be disastrous.

> A seminar participant, Kelly, once began a presentation by standing behind the lectern and staring seriously out at the audience. Kelly then slowly moved around the podium and stood in front of the speaker's table. He pointed out at his audience and declared, "Remember this!"
> Kelly's stern face then turned ashen, and his imperiously pointed finger became limp, as he had completely forgotten the line in his speech that followed "remember this."
> It is one thing to forget a line, but it is far more humiliating to do so immediately after saying, "Remember this."

When words are forgotten in a memorized presentation, the speaker is doomed. People memorize speeches in a word sequence. That is, people— unless they are willing to put the time into the memorizations that professional performers expend—tend to memorize the sequencing of the statement with less than the appropriate regard for the meanings behind the words. Therefore, if the place is lost, so are the speakers because in terms of content, there are few clues as to where they are in the presentation.

If a speaker gives the same exact speech over and over again to different audiences, then a memorized speech is not such a bad idea. First of all, inevitably the speech will become memorized. Secondly, by virtue of the repeated performance the speaker will become intimate with the content of the speech as opposed to just the order of the statements. As a rule, however, people who give presentations infrequently should not memorize speeches. Too many factors are likely to negatively affect the decoding process.

Extemporaneous and Manuscript Formats

Both the extemporaneous and manuscript formats can be appropriate with each having advantages and disadvantages. Which one to use depends on the situation.

Extemporaneous presentations have some advantages over the manuscript format. In general, the extemporaneous speech affords much more flexibility. Extemporaneous speakers have the option of moving away from the lectern, and can move toward or away from sections of the audience as appropriate. Extemporaneous speeches tend to create a more informal atmosphere than the one created in manuscript presentations, and there are times when such informality is absolutely required. Trainers, for example, could not give a manuscript speech and still maintain the appropriate participant-trainer atmosphere necessary for effective teaching and learning.

There are two other benefits of using the extemporaneous approach. One is that there is the *potential* and the *capacity* for more eye contact, though there is certainly no guarantee that such eye contact will occur.

Those who are nervous and unwilling to look into the eyes of the receivers will find some inanimate object on which to focus their attention. I have seen speeches delivered to windows, air conditioners, shoes, ceilings, and finger nails.

The purpose of eye contact is to establish rapport with the audience, and it is essential to have sustained eye contact often enough to obtain such rapport. Many beginning speakers attempt to "finesse" this speaking requirement by snapping their heads up periodically, as if to meet a certain quota of "eye contacts" for the presentation. There is little value in rocketing your face north every twenty seconds or so during a presentation. The value of eye contact is derived from creating a meaningful oculesic bond.

The reason people have difficulty with eye contact is simple. Beginning speakers, in particular, fear the reaction that their words are having. By not looking at the audience, they avoid the possibility that they will notice an uninterested consumer of their message, or worse, a receiver whose facial expressions indicate disdain.

As mentioned in Chapter 5, facial expressions are difficult to accurately decode, but they are decoded regardless. Beginning speakers are often afraid of the nonverbal messages that they may receive and, therefore, avoid looking at the audience. The cure for this malady is twofold: a simple determination to improve eye contact coupled with experience in public speaking. Focusing on some spot on the wall, or cluster of faces, may work at times, but it may well look like the speaker is only looking at a spot on the wall or into clusters of faces.

The last advantage of extemporaneous presentations is a communication phenomenon called *feedback induced response.*

When any communicator in any communication context speaks to a receiver, the communicator (source) is likely to glean feedback in the form of nonverbal messages from the receiver. On the basis of this feedback the source may alter a forthcoming message. Feedback induced response refers to any response that is induced by the source's perception of nonverbal feedback.

In public speaking situations, a good speaker attempts to accurately read the audience and assess how the presentation is going. In extemporaneous presentations, the speaker has the flexibility to alter both the content and the delivery of the message on the basis of this feedback. This is a very real advantage for the comfortable speaker. The beginning speaker is likely not to be calm enough to take advantage of this. However, the ability to cut material, use an anecdote for illustration, or alter in any way the prepared presentation to meet the needs of the audience is advantageous and improves the chances for effective communication.

Despite the advantages of the extemporaneous format some speakers will deliver nothing but manuscript speeches. Melvin Grayson, the director of public relations for the Nabisco corporation, is one such person. Grayson comments:

> I have a horror of extemporaneous speeches, whether I'm speaker or speakee. I don't like to listen to them, because they're

invariably dull and studded with platitudes, not to mention "ers" and "ahs"...I don't like to give [extemporaneous] speeches because of the fear that, while groping for the right phrase, I may deliver the wrong phrase—some remark that will come back to haunt me...As corporate communicators, we sometimes forget—whether we're communicating orally or on paper—the immense significance of each word we use. Yet those words are our weapons; our only weapons...The right words strung together in the right way are what separate a good speech—an effective speech—from one that's a waste of everyone's time. Or worse.

Although there are times when extemporaneous speeches are appropriately utilized, Mr. Grayson is correct about much of what he says. The advantages of manuscript speaking are significant and important to consider.

The primary advantage of manuscript style presentations is that this format allows the speaker the opportunity to prepare as comprehensively as possible for the presentation. When a presentation is written out word for word, the conscientious speaker works on the language of the speech well before the presentation. Extemporaneous formats do not afford such luxury, since the speakers must find the appropriate words while presenting.

In addition, in terms of "pre-game" planning, the preparation for the manuscript speech can include paralingual and oculesic strategies. A speaker can decide what words need emphasis, which sentences require a rapid delivery, which sections should be delivered in soft tones, and what moments would be most appropriate for pauses and eye contact.

Although a hazard in manuscript speaking is the potential for the speech to be read and not delivered, there is no reason why manuscript speeches cannot be delivered forcefully with all the paralingual variations that make a speech successful. Also, by their very nature, manuscript presentations are devoid of pervasive interjections. Whereas extemporaneous speakers might infuse multiple "ers," "ahs," and "ums" in their talks and not even be aware of it, manuscript speakers will not include an annoying abundance of these interjections, since these speakers will not write "er," "ah," and "um" in the manuscript. There may be a tendency for a few interjections at the tail end of some sentences, but for the most part the format eliminates the concern for interjections.

Timing concerns, a crucial factor in public presentations, are also eliminated by the manuscript format. Audiences prepare themselves for presentations of certain lengths. If a speaker goes beyond the expected time limit for the speech, audience members tend to get restless and in general lose their concentration. By the same token, if speakers speak for less than the time length expected, the audience will be unprepared for what will appear to be an abrupt conclusion.

Timing a manuscript speech is relatively easy. In extemporaneous formats one follows an outline and might find that more or less time than expected is needed to convey a certain idea. Also, extemporaneous speaking can lead to speaker digressions, with the result that a speaker might be forced to leave out certain sections as time runs short. Extemporaneous speakers might also simply omit certain sections that they had planned to include. In manuscript speaking, prepared speakers will possibly, but unlikely, skip important sections or be forced because of time constraints to rush conclusions.

Lastly, there are certain times when one must, because of the magnitude of the moment, deliver a manuscript speech. International figures often give manuscript speeches, because the world is hanging on every word that is uttered. The world press is ready to jump on any faux pas, and therefore, it is essential to get it exactly right or suffer the consequences.

During the Carter presidency, Jimmy Carter delivered a speech in Poland in which he remarked that Americans wanted to get to know Polish desires. The speech was a manuscript presentation, but it was being translated simultaneously for the Polish people by an American interpreter. The interpreter, when translating the word "desire," selected a Polish verb that meant "lusts." Carter's statement, therefore, came out as if Americans wanted to get to know Polish "lusts," as if the Poles had a distinctive Eastern brand of fantasies and Americans were curious. Journalists had a party with this error.

On October 22, 1962 during President Kennedy's stirring Cuban Missile Crisis speech, the president used the word "quarantine" to describe his decision to blockade Cuba. Notably, he did not select the word "blockade." This word, he feared, would sound more bellicose than "quarantine" and he wanted to do nothing to exacerbate an already volatile situation.

In order to select an appropriate presentation style then, the following is recommended:

Unless there is no alternative, do not give impromptu speeches. Similarly, memorized speeches are a problem, and as often as not can result in disaster unless a speaker is intimately familiar with the content. In deciding between the other two choices, remember that there are certain contexts that proscribe one or the other of these options. In these scenarios, then, there is no bona fide option. In the case where such an option does exist, beginning speakers who are willing to put in the necessary preparation time for writing the speech and practicing delivery should try the manuscript format because it allows for total control of the message. Experienced speakers, in those contexts that permit it, should try the extemporaneous approach because of the flexibility afforded in these presentations.

STRUCTURING CONTENT

Every presentation ought to be structured to include an introduction, body, and conclusion. In addition, many presentations include a question-and-answer session following the speech.

Introduction

The introduction to a presentation is a crucial part of the speech. It can be a determining factor in the success of the presentation, as it will affect the extent to which the receivers attend to the message. Introductions should contain a statement of purpose, a persuasive hook, and a recognition of the importance of ethos which is an extremely powerful communication factor.

Statement of Purpose. In the beginning of the speech, although not necessarily the very first words that a speaker utters, a speaker is obliged to make some statement indicating the objectives of the presentation. This is particularly important in business presentations. The specific intent of the speaker ought to be clear from the outset.

In essence, the presenter establishes a contract with the audience in the introduction of the presentation promising to meet certain goals. At the end of the presentation, the receivers can evaluate the message on the basis of the goals that the speaker claimed would be met.

Persuasive Hook. In addition to the statement of purpose, the speaker needs to hook the audience at the outset. In some way, the audience needs to be convinced to listen to the presentation. This factor is especially important when the collective receivers did not choose to attend the presentation on the basis of the advertised speech content. Also, this factor becomes particularly relevant when receivers are prepared to listen to a number of speakers all speaking on the same general theme.

Audiences can be difficult to reach. The speaker has the advantage in public speaking contexts of being able to prepare for the audience, but the speaker in this context also has the disadvantage of having to reach a large number of receivers, all with disparate interests, attitudes, and backgrounds.

In addition, people are (as a rule) notoriously poor listeners. People are more adept at feigning attention than actually being attentive. Listeners can contemplate luscious repasts or carnal pleasures while appearing to listen to a presentation about company safety procedures. People are even skilled at nonverbally indicating their attention while not missing a beat with their pleasant reveries. Audience members on distant planets will occasionally grease up their necks and nod sagely when it seems appropriate.

To decrease the numbers who will cerebrally vacate the premises, a speaker needs to convince the audience that it is worth their while to cerebrally stay put. Generally, a good way to hook an audience is to convince them that there is a bona fide need to listen. As long as this need is genuine and not contrived, the speaker is likely to increase attention to the extent that attention can be increased.

A warning with regard to persuasive hooks in introductions: some speakers attempt to hook the audience by asking the audience a question. This is a hazardous strategy. It is not wise to begin a presentation with a question unless that inquiry is a rhetorical question. Audience members will often not respond to the simplest questions when asked to do so.

Recently, a seminar participant, Lane, began a manuscript presentation about money market funds by asking twenty-five business people, "How many of you would like to make more money?"

To this simple query only two people raised their hands. One of them did so as if his arm was encased in cement. Lane was nonplused, as the next line in the text was supposed to be, "Well, since all of you are interested in making money, may I suggest an excellent new money-market fund that is guaranteed to increase your personal treasury." Because of the lack of response to the question, the second line did not follow, so Lane found herself stammering as she clumsily offered, "Er, perhaps some day you will want to make money, and uh, then, I have this good idea." Lane's rhythm was ruined. She muddled through the presentation and when she finished, she was embarrassed and, even a bit angry. "Who doesn't want to make money?" she muttered as she took her seat.

Everybody wants to make money, but not all people will respond to a speaker's question in the manner they expect. If a speaker were to ask twenty-five people if they were breathing at the beginning of the speech, the speaker would be lucky if thirteen people would raise their hands.

Hook the audience with a statement that will convince them that they need to listen, and then follow through.

Ethos Factor. *Ethos* is a crucial communication factor. It refers to the status that is attributed to the speaker by those in the audience. As Richard Nixon painfully discovered in 1974, there is nothing more important to a speaker than ethos. During the height of the Watergate era, President Nixon had a significant credibility problem that severely hampered his ability to govern.

There are three types of ethos: initial ethos, intermediate ethos, and terminal ethos.

Initial ethos refers to that status attributed to a speaker before a sound is uttered in front of the audience. Obviously this initial ethos is a function of speaker appearance and speaker reputation.

Intermediate ethos is the attributed status that fluctuates during the course of a presentation. It is the presenter's personal Dow Jones average that will go up or down depending on a number of factors. Fluid delivery will go a long way to increasing intermediate ethos. As discussed in the section on paralanguage in Chapter 5, a smooth delivery will often effectively counteract thin content. The content itself, of course, can affect intermediate ethos. If a well-groomed and intelligent looking unknown (high initial ethos) began speaking about personnel matters, and then mentioned that his approach to weak links is to schedule floggings for transgressors, I should hope that this speaker's intermediate ethos would tumble.

Lastly, intermediate ethos is affected when a speaker, less than diplomatically, presents a position that the audience considers horrible. For example, if I were speaking in front of a group of Democrats trying to convince them to consider voting Republican in a particular campaign, it would not be wise for me to comment that I felt that anyone who ever voted for Democrats was a sick and sorry human specimen.

Because of the importance of intermediate ethos and related factors, it is essential to comprehensively analyze the audience prior to delivering a speech to assess—to the extent that one can—the nature of the group to whom the message will be addressed.

The last type of ethos is *terminal ethos*. This refers to the ethos a speaker is attributed at the conclusion of the speech. It is often a function of the collective ethos accrued at the end of the presentation and the conclusion to the speech. Terminal ethos is very important to anyone who suspects that there might be a return engagement with a particular audience or members from that audience. Terminal ethos directly affects the speaker's initial ethos in subsequent presentations.

As it relates to ethos and the introduction, speakers should take great pains to do anything they can in terms of delivery, content, and perspective to enhance the likelihood of being attributed high ethos. If managers want to convince employees that they ought to give blood, they should mention that they have given blood. If you want to convince people to buy a certain printer, you should explain that you have no vested interested in printers at the present time (assuming this is true), but that you used to work with a variety of printers and are sure that the LXB 1000 is the best that money can buy.

In sum, the introduction to a speech needs to grab audience attention, specify the presentation objectives, and assist the speaker by increasing the likelihood that speaker ethos will be high.

Body

The body of the speech is the easiest aspect to explain. In the body, speakers simply do what they have set out to do. The old speaker's aphorism goes, "You tell 'em what you're going to tell 'em, you tell 'em, and then you tell 'em what you just told 'em." This is certainly a rather skeletal description of the speech structuring process. However, in the body of the speech, the speaker should simply "tell 'em what you said you'd tell 'em." (At the end of the chapter, methods of constructing persuasive content will be presented.)

As it relates to the presentation of information in the body of the speech, a comment on the benefits of visual aids and handouts that might be used in presentations is appropriate.

The purpose of using visual aids is to facilitate the accurate receipt of information. Often, visual aids can assist in the presentation and receipt of information. The rule is to use visual aids when their usage is *indeed* an aid to the presentation and receipt of information and not to use them when they are counterproductive.

There is an asterisk to this rule of thumb, however, which is particularly relevant to business presentations. In many business contexts, it is assumed the prepared speaker will come to the presentation with handouts for the members of the audience. Sometimes handouts can be valuable in facilitating effective receipt of messages. Sometimes handouts can be distracting, and speakers will find themselves competing with intriguing diagrams that receivers have in front of them.

Nevertheless, since it has become the norm for business presenters to be equipped with handouts, speakers run the risk of a loss in ethos by not preparing the handouts, even if these packets do not inherently enhance the quality of the presentation. Indirectly, they do enhance the quality of the presentation, because otherwise the credibility of speakers as bona fide professionals might be questioned. After all, what is communicated is that which is received. That which is received is a function of many factors, including audience preconceptions of what is appropriate, including handouts.

Speakers will often tell the audience that a handout is a summary of information and to refer to the material later. Sometimes speakers will mention that at certain intervals the materials in front of each audience member will be referred to, and request that until such references are made, participants refrain from looking through the material.

There are a few points to emphasize about the use of visual aids. First, visual aids should enhance, directly or indirectly, the receipt of information. Second, speakers must practice with the visual aid before the time of the actual presentation. Murphy's Law runs rampant with various types of charts and equipment. If a chart can come crashing to the floor, it will. If an overhead projector can have a mechanical failure, it will. If an electrical cord needs to reach twelve feet, it will reach nine feet, and there will not be an extension chord in the vicinity.

Third, speakers should be sure that visuals are visible to all those attending the presentation, regardless of the graphic device used. The query, "Can everyone see this?" is valueless unless everyone can. Some equipment can be moved about to allow for all audience members to have a good angle on the visual. However, if material is written in letters that are too small and the aid cannot be "adjusted," its use will have a detrimental effect on the presentation.

Fourth, speakers should make sure that a potentially distracting visual is not visible until it is time to refer to it. Along the same lines, the visual should be placed so it will not physically block the speaker.

Fifth, visuals should be proofread very carefully. Very little is more humiliating than a misspelled word on a large visual aid.

Conclusion

The conclusion to the speech is crucial. At the end of a speech the speakers should provide a sense of closure for the audience. Too many presentations end with speakers scanning notes and then lifting up, in order to say, "Well, that's about it. Can I take any questions?"

"That's about it" does not make a strong conclusion. Such remarks are likely to damage the speakers' terminal ethos, and they do not provide for the kind of closure that is necessary.

In addition to the "That's about it" syndrome, speakers sometimes conclude presentations by dropping their voices to an inaudible level while rushing from the lectern as if they are late for a train. Physically, visually, paralingually, and verbally a speech has to have a strong conclusion.

There are four strategies that can be used to effectively conclude speeches. Combinations of these approaches can work as well.

Summary. The summary approach is not only the easiest approach, it is also a very good idea, particularly in business presentations. A recapitulation of the key points in the presentation, perhaps complemented with a chart that lists these points, not only provides closure, but emphasizes the main points in the presentation.

Challenge. The challenge method of concluding speeches can also be effective. (For example, "I urge you to pursue this humanitarian cause, and give blood when we have our company blood drive.") Challenges work well in speeches with persuasive content.

Issuing a Probing Question. In this case the speaker ends the presentation by leaving the audience with a question to ponder. The question summarizes the theme of the presentation. (For example, "And so I ask you, if your brother needed blood, would you not want the resources to be there so that your sibling might live?")

Using a Quotation. A quotation that captures the essence of the message can be another effective way of concluding the presentation. In the words of Brendan Francis, "A quotation in a speech, article, or book is like a rifle in the hands of an infantryman. It speaks with authority."

QUESTIONS AND ANSWERS

At the conclusion of presentations, speakers often ask for questions. This is an important time, because if there is a question-and-answer session, the presentation is not really over until the questions have been answered. The speech may have been concluded, but the effort has not ended, nor has the book been closed on your message or ethos until the last question has been answered. Therefore, it is important to deal carefully with questions.

Despite the fact that the questioning period is an important part of the presentation, it is remarkable how poorly many speakers—good and bad—handle these inquiries. Many times I have heard speakers who had done well enough during the formal presentation butcher their efforts by handling questions with all the aplomb and wisdom of a bumbling philistine. In these cases, the speaker apparently has not recognized the importance of the question session and simply has not prepared for it.

Given the difficulties many people have dealing with questions, the following suggestions provide the foundation for improvement. The suggestions fall into two categories: planning for the questioning session and strategies for responding to the questions.

Speakers can do a number of things to prepare for question sessions, including:

- Anticipating potential questions
- Formulating mini-speeches as responses to anticipated questions
- Comprehensively researching the subject
- Preparing for ego-involved responses

Anticipate Probable Questions

The wisest preliminary planning is to anticipate the questions that might be posed during the question session. A good strategy is to examine the speech and identify a number of items that are potential areas for questioning. For each item, actually write out the various questions relating to that item that could be posed.

Of course, only the Amazing Kreskin can predict with certainty all of the questions that might surface. However, a careful approach will yield a number of questions that might surface. Oliver North and his attorney, Brendan Sullivan, were brilliant in this regard during the Contra hearings. Evidently Sullivan and North had considered the senators' possible queries and had worked on responses to those questions.

Formulate Mini-Speeches

A good strategy is to consider not only the potential questions but appropriate responses to those questions. Those prepared responses likely would be in an extemporaneous outline format. However, I have known some businesspeople who actually write out in manuscript form their responses to anticipated questions. Well-prepared politicians do this before press conferences and debates. Their staffs will anticipate questions and may write out the appropriate responses to those questions.

Comprehensively Research the Subject

Since it is impossible to completely predict all questions that might be asked, speakers should become as expert as possible regarding the content of the presentation. I have witnessed a number of disastrous situations in which speaker reputations were destroyed because they could not respond to *basic* questions.

In these cases the formal presentation indicated that the speakers were indeed expert or at least knowledgeable on the subject. However, their inability to answer simple questions revealed that they were familiar only with a prepared presentation text and not the substance of the subject. The credibility attached to not only the speakers, but to the material the speakers had presented was severely affected.

Know Yourself and Avoid Counterproductive Reactions

Speakers tend to get "ego involved" in question-and-answer sessions. That is, there are speakers who take each question as a challenge to their being, and respond as if they are being so challenged. Certainly, there are times when audience members will be pugnacious with their queries. For some speakers, however, all queries are perceived as belligerent attacks. Speakers must know themselves and resolve not to let their egos interfere with the process of responding to questions.

This is difficult for some people. For those who simply cannot see that questions are not always challenges, there is little that can be suggested in the way of remedy. For those less defensive, the suggestion is to be aware of the potential for counterproductive, ego-involved reactions to questions. Such awareness will assist in the answering process and allow these speaker to follow the recommendations.

During the Session: Strategies for Handling Questions

Step 1: Repeat the question.

The number one problem with most people in question-and-answer sessions is that they do not repeat the essence of the posed question. To not do so is both rude and foolish. There are a number of reasons to repeat the essence of the question.

Simple Audibility Problems. Sometimes a question is asked in such a soft voice that no one but the people surrounding the questioner can hear the query. The ensuing response is, therefore, meaningless to most of the audience. Some audience members may attempt to nudge their colleagues and inquire about the nature of the question. Some, however, are content to be excluded, and distracting audience noise is the inevitable result. If a speaker is including a question-and-answer session in the presentation, then there is a desire to have the audience participate in the discussion. All too often question-and-answer sessions digress to private dialogues between inquirer and respondent. By allowing all to hear the question, the response should become a presentation to all that are in the room.

The query, "Can you all hear that?" is almost valueless. Not everyone who cannot hear the question will respond honestly to the question. Unless the presentation is taking place with a small audience, the chances are good that everyone cannot hear the question. Even in small rooms with few attendees, a softly spoken question from the front row will be difficult to hear by those in the back. Speakers should not insult those in the audience by disregarding them. Bring the question to everyone by repeating it so all can hear it.

Repeating the Question "Buys" Time. A questioner might state the following:

> (Question)—"On the basis of your presentation I am led to believe that you support participatory decision making in management. Have you read *Theory Z*? If so, what is your reaction to that book?"

Perhaps it has been quite some time since you've read *Theory Z*. Perhaps you never heard of *Theory Z*. Perhaps you've heard of *Theory Z*, but can't recall the correlation of participatory decision making and the book's posture on the same subject. By repeating the question, you allow yourself some time to formulate as intelligent a response as possible, given the nature of the query.

> (Answer)—"The question is, 'Given my perspective, do I agree with the positions expressed in the book *Theory Z*?' While I have read much about management styles, I confess to not having read the book *Theory Z* completely, but am somewhat familiar with the author's orientation. My understanding is that the theory is essentially a hybrid of Theories X and Y. As such, my attitudes regarding delegating responsibility for decisions would be consistent with the philosophy of the author."

Repeating the Question Allows the Speaker to Make Sense out of an Unwieldy Question. Sometimes audience participants can ask questions that are absurdly convoluted. A good speaker will not ridicule the questioner, even though the question may be ridiculously cumbersome. A good speaker will simply "find" the question, if possible, and repeat it so that the audience will understand the focus of the response. For example:

> (Question)—"I think I have a handle on what you're saying, because it seems to me that when I was with Kodak there was a similar type of situation. However, given the nature of today's 1990s employee can we still, during this particular time frame— and I recognize that this is no longer the 'Me Decade' but another decade, and I also recognize the legacy of the Carter presidency, and even Watergate for that matter, on this stuff—but can we continue to do the same thing now given all that's transpired, historically-wise and politically-wise, you know?"

> (Repetition)—"The question was, 'Given the changes that have taken place over the last decade, can we still effectively use my suggestions for management?'"

By repeating the question, the speaker provided a semblance of respect for the question and created a framework for an intelligent response.

Repeating the Question Allows the Speaker to Change It Subtly.
Assume a question is asked that the speaker does not want to answer. By
changing the question slightly in repetition, the speaker can create a hook
onto which the response can be focused.

This is not easy to do. Persistent questioners might recognize the dodge
and may ask a follow-up question. However, skilled speakers are capable of
such sleight of hand and, particularly when dealing with a hostile audience
whose whole purpose is to topple the speaker, can use this method
effectively. For example:

> (Question)—"Given your position in support of corporate
> training aren't you essentially encouraging early retirement, and
> saying, 'To hell with the veterans. Let's push them out with a group
> of inefficient babes.'"

> (Answer)—"The questioner asks me to comment about my
> position regarding training and how it will affect veteran employ-
> ees. My posture on training is basic. We must train employees to
> be better equipped to handle our new technology. This refers to
> veterans as well as others. Are there any other questions?"

Step 2: After repeating question, direct the answer to everyone.

The speaker should direct the response to the entire audience. In this
way the speaker significantly reduces the chances of the response taking the
form of a dialogue. In fact, the repetition of the question itself should be
directed to the entire audience. While throughout the course of the response,
and at the conclusion of the response, the speaker should make occasional
eye contact with the questioner, the speaker should otherwise have the same
eye contact with the audience during question and answer as during the
formal presentation.

As a rule, one follow-up question should be allowed. ("Follow-up
questions" here do not refer to related queries from other audience participants.) After one, however, your presentation is likely to digress into an
interpersonal conversation. You might invite tenacious questioners to see
you at the conclusion of the meeting, if they would like to continue the
discussion.

Step 3: Maintain a professional tone. Do not debate or deride.

As intimated previously, questioners can ask foolish questions and
there are times when an incisive retort would be most desirable. Often,
questioners do not ask questions at all, but rather use the "floor" as an
opportunity to espouse unrelated philosophies. It is tempting to confront
these speakers on this behavior. In addition, there are instances when
questioners make statements, not to posture—the statements are to the
point—but their remarks are still not questions, only statements. At these
moments, it is enticing to react with a short, "Well, what's the question? Do
you have a question, please?"

To these enticements, restraint is urged. There is nothing to be gained by disparaging questioners. While speakers might get a boff out of sympathetic audience members, it is not worth the minuscule short-term value of such sympathy. Instead, take the high road and do not let your ego get in the way.

Step 4: Conclude the question-and-answer session smoothly.

There ought to be a designated time for questions and answers. Even the most careful speaker will be unable to keep audience attention for too long during question-and-answer sessions. Therefore, after a number of questions have been addressed, the speaker should indicate that one or two more will be taken, and then attempt to end the session after addressing a question comfortably. After answering the last question, the speaker should summarize the thrust of the presentation very briefly, and thank the listeners for their attention.

In conclusion, as it relates to questions and answers, prior to the presentation:

- Anticipate possible questions
- Prepare responses to anticipated questions
- Research exhaustively
- Prepare for the possibility of defensive retorts

When responding to questions:

- Repeat the essence of the questions
- Address responses to entire audience
- Resist temptations to debate
- Conclude in a timely fashion

PERSUASIVE MESSAGES

Melvin Grayson, quoted earlier, once remarked, "The pen may not always be mightier than the sword, but no country ever took up the sword without first having been convinced it should do so."

In organizations as well as in national politics, the ability to persuade others is an essential management goal. Many presentations are persuasive in nature and it is important to understand the elements of persuasion.

When people try to persuade others, they are attempting to do one of four basic things. Persuaders attempt to:

- Influence others to consider changing behavior or attitudes
- Change behavior or attitudes
- Reaffirm existing behavior or attitudes
- Actuate—get people to act

Persuasion often involves combinations of these goals. You might want to influence someone to consider changing an attitude and then subsequently attempt to convince them to do something on the basis of their newly held belief.

Any communicative *attempt* to facilitate meeting one or more of these goals is a persuasive attempt. The only such attempt that would *not* be considered persuasion would be one that did not allow the receivers a genuine perception of choice.

It is not persuasion to threaten to smash another's head with a mallet if they decide not to buy your product or service. That is coercion, not persuasion. The persons being persuaded (receivers) must have a genuine perception of choice.

The key question to ask is: What facilitates persuasion? That is, what methods are most effective in helping those who persuade reach their goals? The strategies discussed in the following sections address this question.

Persuasive Approaches

The foundation for any persuasive attempt is the persuader's knowledge of the audience. The more the speaker can find out about the demographics and attitudes of the receivers, the better off the speaker is in preparing to persuade them. Once the speaker has discovered as much as possible about the audience, the following content strategies are suggested.

Use of Yourself as a Credible Source. These arguments are called arguments of ethos. As discussed previously, ethos refers to the status that receivers attribute to those people who speak to them or, as it relates to this material, to those people who attempt to persuade them. I reiterate that nothing is more important to a persuasive speaker than ethos. Once credibility is forsaken, persuading someone that the earth is round is difficult.

As Abraham Lincoln commented many years ago, "If once you forfeit the confidence of your fellow citizen, you can never regain their respect and esteem."

Simply, who you are is often perceived as more important than the logical or emotional impact of any other arguments you might employ. For this reason, advertisers frequently seek actors and athletes to sell their goods. It is no accident that Robert Young, the actor who played the omniscient father in the TV series "Father Knows Best" and the sage physician Marcus Welby in the program of the same name, was involved in a number of Sanka commercials. Would Jim Anderson or Marcus Welby steer us wrong?

Similarly, any individual who develops a reputation for wisdom and honesty can often persuade by relying heavily on that reputation. For this reason, and others, persuading honestly is a wise practice.

Logical Arguments. Persuasion that attempts to convince the receivers that it makes sense to do what the persuader is suggesting is often successful. The persuader should attempt to illustrate, using financial, political, or even social information that there is a logical reason to change one's behavior.

The goal with this strategy is to have the receiver think that it is logical to behave in a certain way. If an employee suggests that a department package a product in a new, more cost-effective way, the employee is trying to reach the rational spot in the receiver that is receptive to that type of logic. Simply, "This packaging strategy can save us money. If this strategy is as sound in other ways as our prior policy, then we should use this strategy and use the extra savings for other projects."

If I suggest that signing up for a series of workshops will have specific long-range value, I am appealing to my receivers to think logically about my product and the merit of education.

Not all "logical arguments" are indeed logical. The history of advertising, for example, is full of persuasive campaigns that used "logical" argumentation that, under scrutiny, were found not to be logical at all. A soup company once tried to persuade consumers to buy their vegetable soup product by visually illustrating the huge amount of vegetables in the soup. Pictures of the soup made the broth look as if it was brimming with all types of wonderful vegetables. An examination, however, revealed that the persuaders had placed marbles on the bottom of the soup bowl to force the relatively few vegetables to the surface of the bowl.

The "logic" of this persuasion was,

- One can see that one will get plenty of vegetables with this soup.
- No one wants soup that requires a search party for the legumes.
- Therefore, buy our product, which is loaded with vegetables.

This is a clear example of a "logical argument," because it attempted to get receivers to *think* that the argument being made was logical. It is also a clear example of a logical argument that is *not* particularly logical.

Emotional Arguments. A very effective method of persuasion is the one that attempts to engage the emotions of those being persuaded. Persuasive messages that involve sympathy, fear (still allowing the receiver a genuine perception of choice), guilt, humor, and intimations of physical pleasure are often extremely successful. The most cursory review of persuasive campaigns would indicate that this emotional strategy is used quite frequently, often complementing logical strategies.

Campaigns for charitable causes, insurance needs, cosmetic products, and even toothpaste include these emotional arguments. Few people over thirty can forget the toothpaste product whose sales rose dramatically when it began claiming that this toothpaste had "sex appeal." In interpersonal persuasion, people often successfully persuade by making their receivers feel guilty, fearful, or excited about the prospects of accepting the persuasive proposal.

Use of Reservations. Any persuasive effort has an opposing side. The arguments that are the arsenal for the opposing side are called reservations. Effective persuasion takes into consideration these reservations. One can effectively incorporate the reservations into his or her persuasive effort by doing one of three things with each reservation:

• One should refute the reservation outright if the counterargument is refutable.
• If the reservation is not refutable, then one should downplay the significance of the reservation. For example,

> "While it is true that person X will cost you less to hire than I will, person X does not have nearly the experience and concomitant expertise that I have, and therefore it makes sense to hire me. I'd come more expensive, but I'd be a better value."

• The last resort in dealing with reservations is to ignore the reservation in your persuasion. It *is* a *last resort*. The only reason one should rely on this last resort is if the reservation is truly insignificant *and* one's best guess is that very few, if any, receivers will have thought of it.

One last comment regarding content strategies in persuasion. This comment relates to ethical considerations and persuasion. Simply, there are two basic routes one can take when persuading. One route is to say, "Never mind ethics. Let the receivers/customer beware. It is fine to say anything in order to persuade another."

The other route is to use valid arguments when persuading. For two simple reasons the valid route is strongly recommended. As mentioned previously, dishonest persuasion makes subsequent persuasive efforts more difficult. A persuader might be able to short cut persuasion by deceiving once or twice, but in the long run the persuader's "ethos" is damaged and persuasion becomes very difficult. Adlai Stevenson once commented, "He who slings mud, usually loses ground."

Also, at one point or another we are all in the position of being receivers. Never have I ever met anyone who enjoyed being duped. If you bought an inefficient car, and subsequently discovered that the salesperson knew it was a lemon when you bought the auto, it is highly unlikely that you would return to the dealer and say to the salesperson, "You sly fox! That was very clever of you, convincing me to buy that old lemon. Very good. Very good."

That such "unethical" persuasion is normal certainly cannot be refuted. In writing and teaching about persuasion, however, I emphasize that for pragmatic and ethical considerations persuaders are wise to be honest.

Summary Regarding Persuasion

Successful persuasion is facilitated by an accurate analysis of the nature of one's audience and the implementation of intelligent argumentative strategies.

The recognition of the importance of speaker reputation is an extremely important understanding for those who persuade. The incorporation of logical and emotional arguments into persuasive efforts will increase the likelihood of persuasive success. Lastly, the ability to effectively, visually and vocally, deliver persuasive content will enhance the likelihood of reaching one's persuasive goals.

STAGEFRIGHT

One of the bigger problems involved in presentations is the sheer terror of giving a presentation. Magazines often publish articles about people's fear of public speaking. In the summer 1980 issue of the *Saturday Evening Post*, for example, an article appeared titled, "Public Speaking and Other Coronary Threats." Speaking anxiety is a remarkable phenomenon. Consider the case of Sandra Winston.

> Sandra Winston enrolled in a speaking skills workshop with me. She told me before the first session that she had never spoken in front of a group before and was "deathly afraid" of doing so. Nevertheless, she wanted to take the course in order to conquer her fears.
>
> On the first day of presentations, Winston rushed to the lectern determined to be the first speaker so, she told me later, she could get it out and get it over with.
>
> The speech began quite well. Shortly after it began, a rude latecomer crashed through the door making a racket like one would hear in a factory. The tardy man glanced around the room looking for a chair, spotted one on the far side of the room and marched right in front of the speaker swinging his coat as he walked past her. In fact, while hustling by Ms. Winston, he swiped the lectern with his jacket.
>
> I was happily surprised to note that the speaker was able to maintain her composure throughout this rudeness. She continued to speak effectively as the tardy man made even more noise while settling into his seat.
>
> At the end of the class, I commented that late seminar participants should wait until each speaker is finished before entering the seminar room. I commented that Winston had done a remarkable job of maintaining her poise despite the noise.
>
> I asked Sandra Winston to stay after class and repeated that I had been impressed with her poise given the rude latecomer.
>
> "How did you keep going?" I inquired.
>
> "I didn't even see him," she immediately replied.

One would have had to have been there to recognize the nature of the feat of being oblivious to this man's noisy entrance. Winston continued to comment that she was so afraid that she absolutely did not see anything during the course of her presentation.

A main reason for stagefright is related to the relative infrequent times that people in our society are called on to deliver speeches. Another reason for speech anxiety, as alluded to in an earlier section of this chapter, is that people fear the nonverbal feedback from the strangers who comprise the audience.

The best way to deal with such apprehension is to realize that it is normal and to try to use that energy for you. Like an actor who is energized, yet nervous, for opening night, the speaker can use the nervous energy to enhance the quality of performance. This strategy is certainly found in the "easier said than done" file. However, the only way to reduce the speech anxiety is to force yourself into repeated speaking situations. As you become more familiar with the nuances of the presentation setting, the anxiety level is likely to dissipate. All managers do not have to make presentations, but when a manager must, it is important to make the best of it.

SUMMARY

In the 1800s, Scottish essayist Thomas Carlyle remarked, "Can there be a more horrible object in existence than an eloquent man not speaking the truth?"

When we think of Adolph Hitler, Carlyle's comment is especially true. While demagogues like Hitler have a more significant impact than the typical corporate manager, it is also chilling to think of managerial careers that have been thwarted because of poor speaking skills. There are many individuals who never "made it" because they could not or would not learn how to speak effectively.

Some people cannot imagine delivering a speech or a presentation. The thought itself is frightening. I guarantee that every person who wants to can become an adequate speaker and make fine presentations in the organizational setting. The suggestions in this chapter coupled with serious practice will yield positive results.

7

Improving Interpersonal Communication

Interpersonal communication is the most prevalent communication context. While people will periodically interact in conferences and occasionally deliver and attend speeches, people engage in multiple dyadic exchanges daily.

It is no different in organizations. Occasionally there are speeches to attend or make—more frequently there are meetings—but employees are constantly involved in interpersonal interactions either on the formal networks or, more commonly, on the informal networks. These interpersonal interactions and the residuals from these exchanges affect productivity, managerial decisions, the nature of relationships within the organization, and, of course, the communication climate (see Chapter 4).

The examination of interpersonal communication is a relatively recent area of investigation in communication study. Until the 1970s, the focus of most scholars' attention was on communication in public speaking or group communication contexts. Because interpersonal exchanges are so common in daily life, many students of communication began to turn their attention to the investigation of those factors that affect interpersonal interaction. The analysis of interpersonal communication is complex. There are many variables affecting the process, and there have been multiple theories offered to explain the nuances of the dyad. Too often, however, theories have been put forth that were nothing short of ethereal, "pie in the sky" solutions to this complex communication context.

In this chapter, therefore, a very pragmatic approach to the analysis of interpersonal communication in the organization will be taken. There will be a presentation of two ways of looking at the dyad. One assists in visualizing the dynamics of the process, and the other is an unusually practical method for improving interpersonal communication in the organization and elsewhere.

RULES APPROACH TO INTERPERSONAL COMMUNICATION

A rules approach to interpersonal communication simply views communication as an act that has a set of rules. Just like Checkers or Monopoly has rules that govern playing, so does communication. These rules determine the success of the interpersonal interaction, and the effect these dyadic exchanges will have on subsequent interactions.

The rules approach may appear simplistic—and it is. However, there is merit to thinking about interpersonal communication in organizations in this manner. Consider the following example:

Example 1: Checkers with a Friend
>   If you were playing Checkers with a friend, and you were to get a piece to the back of your opponent's row, you would likely say "king me" to your opponent. At that point a piece should be taken, placed atop your marker, and you would be "kinged." Assume, however, that the friend did not "king" you. Assume that when you said, "King me," your opponent simply said, "No." The conversation that would ensue might go like this:
>   "What do you mean, no? King me."
>   "I'm not going to. I don't want to."
>   "Are you daft? You're supposed to 'king me' when I get my piece to the back of your row."
>   "I'm not into that today."
>   "Well, forget it then. I'm not playing with you."

In Checkers, such an eventuality is unlikely. In interpersonal communication, however, people "quit" the game often because others have broken the implicit rules that govern the interaction.

The next three examples show how the rules approach applies to interpersonal communication in organizations.

Example 2: McDonald and Barrett
>   Gene McDonald, a mid-level employee, walked into the mailroom to check his box and noticed that a package was sitting on a table addressed to Sandra Barrett. Barrett was a new worker at the PRB Corporation and one of McDonald's peers. McDonald's office cubicle was not far from Barrett's, and he decided to be helpful and bring the package over to the new employee. McDonald took the package from the mailroom, walked onto the office floor, and approached Barrett's desk.

"Sandy," said McDonald. "This came for you. I spotted it in the mailroom."

Barrett took the package, said "thank you" in a clipped paralingual manner, and then commented, "Don't ever call me Sandy, again. My name is Sandra. I'm not a 'Sandy.' Please don't forget it."

McDonald's immediate response was to nod a stunned "okay," and return to his desk. As he told me subsequently, he decided after that encounter never to speak with Sandra Barrett again unless it was absolutely essential. He stated definitively that he wasn't going to call her Sandra, Sandy, or Mudd, unless he had to. McDonald commented that Barrett's remark was gratuitous, and he wanted nothing to do with her after what he perceived to be a rebuke, particularly considering that he'd been doing her a favor when she "accosted" (his word) him.

Example 3: Patterson and the Bank Clerk

Ann Patterson told me that she went to the same bank every other Friday to cash her check. The bank was an old-fashioned sort. Instead of the long serpentine lines that are characteristic of most approaches to the teller windows in modern banks, this bank had single lines in front of individual tellers. Most people waited on the shortest line for service and hoped that their chosen line moved quickly.

Ann Patterson did not typically wait on the shortest line. Patterson waited on the same teller's line every time, because she had grown accustomed to interacting with an anonymous man (referred to as Rapp). According to Patterson, Rapp was efficient. She felt that she had, in the past, wasted time with some of the other "airhead" tellers, so she always would wait for Rapp even if his line was longer than another.

Patterson's interactions with Rapp were almost always the same. A typical conversation might have gone like this.

Patterson: "Hello."
Rapp: "Hi. How are you this week?"
Patterson: "Fine thanks, you?"
Rapp: "Good. No complaints. Just depositing this?"
Patterson: "Yes, that's right."
Rapp: "Alright...here you go. Here's your slip."
Patterson: "Thank you."
Rapp: "Have a good day...Next please."

The conversations were most predictable. On one particular Friday, Ann Patterson approached the window and the interaction changed. In response to the initial "hello" from Patterson, Rapp said "hi," paused, and then while looking at the paperwork blurted, "How's your sex life?"

Rapp then rocketed his head up to see how his attempt had fared. It had not been a grand success. Patterson emitted a stunned, staccato "just fine." She grabbed her deposit slip, left the bank, and never stood in Rapp's line again.

Example 4: The Dean and Me

On my first day as a university professor there was a torrential rainstorm. In consecutive periods on that rainy day I taught two classes. After dismissing the second group, I stayed in the room for a while assessing and enjoying the moment. There was a knock on the classroom door. I looked to my left and saw the door open and my dean enter the classroom.

"Well, how did it go, Alan?" he asked.

I told him it went well, but that was not what I was thinking. I was thinking, and still think, what an extraordinarily considerate gesture for the dean to walk close to a mile from his office on a stormy day to ask how my first class had gone.

In the McDonald and Barrett example Gene McDonald decided "not to play" with Sandra Barrett anymore. In the bank example, Ann Patterson decided "not to play" with Mr. Rapp anymore. In the instance with my Dean and the rainstorm, I thought that he had been very considerate, and my subsequent interactions with him and his staff reflected the way I thought he "played the game."

A problem with communication and rules is that the rules are not written on the back of a box somewhere. People bring with them a bag of rules, which are often not revealed until "game time."

The rules approach helps to visualize what takes place during interpersonal communication. People who can assess the rules and "play" by the rules while not prostituting themselves facilitate the possibilities of effective communication. There are times when someone else's rules must be broken, because to avoid doing so is to be cowardly and will subsequently create internal and likely external problems.

In many instances, however, rules are broken because the parties involved do not take the time to sensitize themselves to the possible rules of the game as the other person defines them. When this happens—as it often does—there can be considerable interpersonal friction.

The key then, is to be sensitive, perceptive, and intelligent in the assessment of the parameters governing interpersonal communications. Unfortunately, even if a manager is aware of this "key," it is difficult to find and train people who can be so sensitive, perceptive, and intelligent.

As the *Wall Street Journal* put it in its July 2, 1985 article about managerial training, "You can't run them [managers] through a charm school and have natural communicators."

TRANSACTIONAL ANALYSIS

In 1961, Eric Berne, a psychotherapist, published a book titled, *Transactional Analysis in Psychotherapy.* The book was essentially designed to explain a self-help process for psychotherapy. Berne's book met with mixed reviews. It was not received positively by many in the psychotherapeutic community and was too academically written for many lay people to understand.

In 1967, Thomas Harris, published a simpler version of Berne's philosophy or approach, titled *I'm O.K., You're O.K.* Four years later, Muriel James and Dorothy Jongeward published *Born to Win,* another book presenting the substance of transactional analysis (TA) in simple form. Both *I'm O.K., You're O.K.* and *Born to Win* sold very well. Transactional analysis became a type of pop phenomenon in the early 1970s, with TA groups meeting throughout the country and TA retreats taking place with surprising, if not alarming, regularity.

The success of Harris's book and James and Jongeward's book spawned additional volumes by entrepreneurial authors who wanted to capitalize on the TA popularity. *TA for Tots* appeared in print, *The O.K. Boss* was published, and Eric Berne himself wrote *What Do I Say After I Say Hello.* Although TA was developed for use in psychotherapy, in the 1970s many communication scholars began to see its applications for the examination of interpersonal communication.

In the presentation of transactional analysis here, I emphasize that there is *no* interest in TA for its possible therapeutic value. Transactional analysis is presented here simply as a model for analyzing interpersonal communication, and more importantly, as a practical tool for *improving* interpersonal communication. For people who want to improve their communications with others in the workplace, or elsewhere, finding a more pragmatic method to facilitate such improvement would be difficult.

The discussion of transactional analysis will include sections on the transaction, ego states, types of transactions, communication modes, scripts, and contracts.

Readers should note that some of the TA language is somewhat trendy and dated. It was written this way, I assume, to make the approach more palatable to those in the 1960s and 1970s who might have found a nonacademic vocabulary more attractive. Also, I am sure, there was an attempt to present the material as simply as possible, as TA was designed as a lay person's tool. I encourage readers of the 1990s not to be put off by the outdated jargon of transactional analysis. The next few pages might contain expressions which are reflective of another era and may be redolent of some "touchy-feely" pop philosophies. However, there is very little "touchy-feely" about the application of TA. In communication contexts, TA is nothing if not a practical model.

The Transaction

Berne uses the term *transaction* because it implies that there is an exchange between the source and receiver. The prefix, *trans-*, means across, and according to Berne something does go "across" from source to receiver when there is an interaction. For practical purposes the transaction is synonymous with what is often called an *interaction.*

Ego States

Transactional analysis is based on examinations or analyses of transactions. In each analysis, there is an assessment made about the nature of the message sent in terms of the *ego state* from which the message emanates. Each person is said to use three ego states. These three are labeled the Parent, Adult, and Child ego states, and are always written with a capital P, A, and C (to distinguish these words from people who have children, are postadolescent, or who are youngsters, that is parents, adults and children).

The *Parent* ego state is characterized by judgmental, nurturing, and/ or admonishing communicative behavior. The *Adult* ego state is characterized by objective and rational communicative behavior. The *Child* ego state is characterized by communicative behavior expected of children. No matter how old or how young, everyone exhibits all three ego states at one time or another.

A key to understanding ego states is that they are *not* theoretical concepts. Ego states are phenomenological realities. They are evident whenever people are engaged in interpersonal interactions (transactions).

For example, when Dave asks a stranger the time, he is coming out of the Adult ego state and is attempting to "hook" the stranger's Adult ego state. That is, Dave is asking a rational question and hopes to get a rational response.

Were Dave to admonish a coworker for a bad job by sporting a scowl while shouting, "That's very bad work, Lou," Dave would be coming out of his Parent ego state, and would likely be trying to "hook" Lou's Child ego state.

If Dave said to his boss, "Come on, Shirley, let's blow the afternoon off," Dave would be coming out of his Child ego state, and hoping to "hook" Shirley's Child ego state.

In the last example, for instance, Dave, speaking as a child, hopes to get a response from Shirley that similarly will be childish, such as, "Okay, let's not work today; let's play."

The determination of whether a message is coming from the Parent, Adult, or Child ego state is made on the basis of the content of the message and the nonverbal factors that accompany the verbal content. Paralingual and oculesic factors, therefore, are part of the determination.

The analyses of transactions are typically diagrammed. For example, the example last cited would be diagrammed as:

P   P

A   A

C ⟷ C

Types of Transactions

There are three types of transactions called the complementary, crossed, and ulterior transactions.

Complementary Transactions. Assume that when Dave asks the stranger "what time is it," the stranger responds by saying that it is "twenty past noon." This exchange would be called a *complementary* transaction, because the ego state Dave attempted to hook was hooked, and the stranger responded to the original ego state. Such a transaction is diagrammed as follows:

The statement, "what time is it," goes Adult to Adult, and the response, "It's twenty past noon," also goes Adult to Adult. Complementary transactions are very simple ones to analyze and, on the surface, they appear to be examples of effective communication. Certainly, that is the case with this basic, noncharged transaction.

Crossed Transactions. Assume, for a moment, that the stranger is not so polite. Assume that the stranger does not tell Dave the time, but responds by glaring and saying, "Fellow, why don't you get yourself a watch. What do I look like, Big Ben?"

This is an example of a *crossed* transaction. Dave would have been rebuked and would not have been successful at finding out the time. That transaction is diagrammed as follows:

Ulterior Transactions. Ulterior transactions are a bit more complicated and are the types of transactions that create insidious problems for the organization. *Ulterior* transactions are by definition deceptive transactions. In these exchanges, people attempt to hook ego states indirectly. That is, deceptive people try to solicit desired responses by manipulating the other person.

For example, consider a scene in which a young boy is in the backyard with his father. The father, in an authoritarian manner commands, "Son, let's get down to work." That statement can be very easily diagrammed as:

A response from the son that would complement this transaction might be, "Sure, Dad, I'll help you, because some day I want to learn how to be big and strong like you."

A response that would result in a crossed transaction might be, "Perhaps we should discuss this matter more carefully before we engage in this particular project."

In these two cases the transactions would be diagrammed as:

Case 1 - Complementary Transaction

Case 2 - Crossed Transaction

However, what if the transaction between father and son goes like this:

Father: "Let's get down to work."
Son: "Sure Dad, I'll help you, because I know you're too old to do it yourself."

This is an instance of an ulterior transaction, because the son makes it appear as if he is attempting to hook the father's Parent, but in reality the son wants to hook the father's Child, and have the father say, "What do you mean, I'm too old to do it myself. Go out and play, and leave me be."

In this way the son has manipulated the father to say what he wants the father to say. This particular ulterior transaction is diagrammed in this way:

Case 3 - Ulterior Transaction

Far too often, people in organizations engage in ulterior transactions while trying to solicit particular responses in order to obtain some payoff. Of course, not all interpersonal exchanges are typically characterized by ulterior transactions. Enough are so characterized, however, to warrant attention to the possibility that our interpersonal exchanges are rooted in deception. Often people do not even realize that they are being deceptive and manipulative when they are interacting.

Communication Modes

Transactional analysis suggests that there are different degrees of substance in interpersonal exchanges, which can be categorized into five communication modes.

Rituals. *Rituals* refer to the most basic communication mode. Sometimes called *phatic communications,* rituals are characterized by small-talk exchanges. A typical ritual exchange would go like this:

"Hi, how are you?"
"Good and you?"
"Fine, thanks."
"Good to see you."
"Thanks. So long."

Sometimes these exchanges take place so rapidly, and are so often uttered by rote that one party does not wait for the appropriate response before offering the next line. A coworker of mine often says, "Fine, thanks" after her "How are you?" regardless of whether I utter a sound.

Ritual transactions are intended more to acknowledge another's existence than anything else. A person who *literally* responded to ritualistic queries would be considered weird indeed.

Imagine the reaction of one colleague who passed another in the office. After he smiled and said, "What's happening?" he was yanked over to a desk to hear, "What's happening? I'll tell you what's happening. I have a bruise on my hip the size of Nebraska that I got from playing tennis with Harvey, and it's killing me. It's absolutely killing me. It hurts every time I take a step. That's what's happening with me."

The reaction to this outburst might well be, "Who asked ya?" The colleague certainly had not. He was involved in a ritual transaction that was meant to acknowledge and not to ignore an acquaintance. He does not want to hear about Harvey and the tennis bruise. In fact, most people engage in rituals precisely because they do not want to get involved in talking in greater detail for one reason or the other. He may be in a hurry, or he may just not want to talk about anything that approaches being substantive.

In the mid-1970s when the running boom was hitting its peak, almost all runners would acknowledge another runner's presence with a ritualistic nonverbal greeting. It is easy for people to say hello to complete strangers even in large cities when they know they are going to be racing right past them momentarily. It is much tougher to engage in substantive interactions for any meaningful duration.

The following example illustrates how limited ritual communication can be.

> Imagine that a person walks into a supermarket, pushes his cart down the aisle, and spots an acquaintance—not a friend, a peripheral acquaintance—walking down the aisle. He is likely to engage in a ritual greeting with this person, whom we will call Charlie.
>
> "Hi Charlie. How are you?"
>
> "Good. Thanks," says Charlie.
>
> He passes the acquaintance, finishes up in aisle one, and turns down aisle two. There again he spots him. This time as Charlie approaches, he might say, "Hi, again."
>
> Charlie might contort his face in a "What do you know?" smile, then chuckle, then mimic, "Hi again," and walk on by.
>
> Down aisle three he goes. He bumps into Charlie a third time and says with a dramatic smile, "We've got to stop meeting like this." Charlie concurs with a playful snort.
>
> He turns down aisle five a few minutes later, and there he is again. This time the person does not want to see Charlie. He has exhausted, "How are you," "Hi again," and "We've got to stop meeting like this." There is very little left in his ritual repertoire. He may well pick up a bottle of ketchup, pretend to scrutinize the ingredients, wait for Charlie to pass by, put the ketchup down, and proceed with his shopping. Both are hopeful that they do not make eye contact in the store again.

Pastimes. *Pastimes* are exchanges that are a notch more substantive than rituals. Discussions about the weather are examples of pastimes. Simply, they are nonsubstantive transactions during which the participants attempt to pass the time.

Withdrawal. *Withdrawal* is a communication mode in which the person who withdraws attempts to avoid any interpersonal transactions. The person, in the extreme case, may be agoraphobic, or in a less serious situation, might simply want to be alone for a particular time.

Games. *Games* refer to a communication mode that is typified by ulterior transactions. Employees and employers who engage in games generally want to manipulate others by communicating deceptively.

As an example, let us say that a manager is less concerned with productivity than maintaining power. By communicating deceptively, the manager may be able to manipulate the employee to continue to play an inappropriately servile role. Likewise, employees can be deceptive in order to ingratiate themselves with top management or get out of certain responsibilities.

Ingenuous Communication. Referred to as "intimacy" in Berne's nomenclature, *ingenuous communication* is defined as open, honest, and as it relates to TA, substantive communication.

An important note to make here is that ingenuous communication may or may not facilitate effective communication. While it is true that some people are taken by ingenuous communicators, others are put off by such communication since it is so unusual.

It is far more common for someone to initiate an interaction with a stranger that he would like to meet by discussing something peripheral, than by stating simply that his approach is due to a physical or other attraction they might have to the other person. In the hope of initiating a conversation, people will approach others in libraries and ask, "What time is it?" despite the fact that there might be six large clocks in the vicinity.

SCRIPTS AND SCRIPTING

Although scripting is the most controversial aspect of TA, it is an important aspect to discuss in order to understand the nature of interpersonal communication problems in organizations. According to Berne, much of what we say does not reflect our own personal beliefs and philosophies. Not only this, but the way we speak (paralingually) and other nonverbal communicative factors are often not our own. He argues that many people as youngsters receive a tremendous number of messages that go Parent to Child. These people do not evaluate the messages they receive in their Child, but simply "ship" these philosophies north to their Adult.

Therefore, when people speak out of their Adult, according to Berne, they often are simply spewing a script that has been written by a host of aunts, neighborhood bullies, clergymen, cops, sports figures, parents, and television personalities, to name a few who have sent messages that never were evaluated by this person.

For example, if Johnny is told and shown that it is okay for coaches to scream at players, but not okay for teachers to scream at students, Johnny may argue at a subsequent date that it is fine for such communicative behavior to be commonplace, out of his Adult ego state. It may be, however, that this philosophy Johnny naturally spews forth never went through his internal processing apparatus.

Obviously, the ramifications of this theory are enormous. It is very difficult to alter the expressions of your own ideas, if your own ideas are not yours but an amalgamation of others.

Certainly, many take issue with Berne over this philosophy. To agree in entirety would be to acknowledge that the world is populated primarily by nonthinking zombies. However, to improve interpersonal communication it is worthwhile to consider the possibility that transactions are a function of scripted input.

CONTRACTS

The "bottom line" in TA is the use of *contracts.* Contracts incorporate all that has been discussed previously in this section of the chapter. They refer to specific methods for improving interpersonal communication with particular others.

To use contracts, a specific interpersonal communication problem must be identified, and a specific TA strategy implemented. The process involves a number of steps.

In the examples used below to illustrate the process for each step, an employee writes in the first person about strategies for changing interpersonal exchanges with a coworker, Williamson:

Step 1. Identify the communication problem and desired communication outcome in TA terminology.

Williamson frequently comes out of his Parent ego state during interactions with me. Too often I find that he is successful in hooking my Child. I do not want that to continue, and want to communicate out of my Adult, with complementary transactions when dealing with Williamson.

Step 2. Specify a strategy to deal with the problem in terms of relevant communication principles.

Typically, these principles are related to the three Vs: *visual, verbal,* and *vocal* factors.

When I interact with Williamson, I am going to cross every transaction that comes at me, Parent to Child with an Adult-Adult response.

Visually, I will attempt to maintain eye contact with Williamson at all times during the transactions. Vocally, I will speak at an even, unexcited paralingual rate. And, verbally, I will select words that will be formal and not casual. I will use no slang.

Step 3. Practice role playing the scenario with a friend.

In this stage I will get an acquaintance to assume Williamson's traits so that I can practice and hone my approach to subsequent communications with the troublesome colleague.

Step 4. Implement strategies in the transactions with Williamson.

I will attempt to do what I have conceived as strategic in order to resolve the communication problem.

Step 5. Play the cerebral "tapes" of the conversations and do a transactional analysis of the interaction.

Often after exchanges we "replay" our conversations with others. While it is difficult to perform such replays precisely, attempt to do so and then actually diagram the exchanges in order to assess the success of the strategy.

Step 6. Go back to Step 2 and reevaluate strategy if necessary.

It is unlikely that after the first attempt all will be copasetic. It is more likely that I will have to reexamine the strategy initially devised. If the strategy is weak, I will alter it appropriately. Probably the strategy will be fine, but I will need more practice with the implementation. This is not the time to say, "Ah the hell with it. I can live with it." Stay the course.

Step 7. Continue with steps through 3 to 6.

Eventually, the coworker will be in a position where he can change the way that he interacts with Williamson. It may be that the entire nature of his relationship with Williamson will change. And it may be that the cost of such a change will be greater than the benefit derived from the increased comfort of the changed nature of the interpersonal communication.

This contract system can work. In organizations and elsewhere, people can decide to change their communicative behavior, and nature of their communicative interactions by "contracting" and practicing such communicative changes. This method of contracting is strongly recommended. It is not nebulous, 1969, bohemian stuff. It can be implemented.

SUMMARY

This chapter focused on the nature of interpersonal communication and methods that can be implemented to improve interpersonal communication in the organization.

A rules approach to interpersonal communication has been presented, which implies that communication is governed by an implicit set of rules. One of the goals of a successful communicator should be the ability to assess the rules that govern each exchange.

The basics of transactional analysis have also been presented as a method for analyzing and changing the nature of interpersonal communication. Transactional analysis provides a pragmatic framework for assessing the nuances of the transaction and a workable strategy for intervention to improve transactions with others.

Managers who work on improving interpersonal communication make their work easier. An initial step, however, prior to implementation of transactional analysis or any other communication strategy, is some genuine introspection.

8

Effective
Conference
Communication

"If Moses had been a committee the Israelites would still be in Egypt."—J.B.Hughes

"A committee is a cul de sac to which ideas are lured and quietly strangled."—John A. Lincoln

"[A committee] is a group of men who keep minutes and waste hours."—Anonymous

"What is a committee? A group of the unwilling, picked from the unfit, to do the unnecessary."—Richard Harkness, *New York Herald Tribune,* June 15, 1960

Conference communication may be the most frustrating of all types of communicating. At one time or another, everyone has been in a meeting that has been exasperating because of the pace of progress, the irresponsibility of the membership, or the apparent meaninglessness of the proceedings.

Nevertheless, particularly in organizations, meetings occur frequently and often seem to usurp all the hours of the day. An executive friend claims that she spends three-fourths of her day in meetings. Her normal routine has her simply moving from one conference room to another, and this daily schedule is not that unusual for top-level and middle-level managers. Administrators spend an inordinate amount of time in conferences.

To some, meetings are seen as a cure all for the communication ills of an organization. Unfortunately, they are not. Actually, meetings often create communication problems for organizations.

Meetings can be valuable methods of disseminating information, and they can be functional conduits for subordinate-to-superior messages. But they should not be construed as the only communication vehicle available, and certainly should not be viewed and utilized as the fail-safe cure all for organizational problems. Indeed, holding a meeting when such a conference is unnecessary or inappropriate is a primary source of subsequent frustration. Satirist Dave Barry's comments in *How to Attend a Meeting* (from *Claw Your Way To the Top*) are both humorous and to the point. He writes,

> [Sometimes] meetings are held for basically the same reason that Arbor Day is observed—namely, tradition. For example, a lot of managerial people like to meet on Monday, because it is Monday...This type of meeting operates the way "Show and Tell" does in nursery school, with everybody getting to say something, the difference being that in nursery school the kids actually have something new to say. When it's your turn, you should say you're still working on whatever it is you're supposed to be working on.

There are those times, however, when meetings are essential. They can be excellent vehicles for information dissemination, group interaction and input, upward message diffusion, and necessary social interaction. The keys, of course, are to meet in groups when appropriate and to structure conferences to facilitate effective interaction.

This chapter suggests six factors that are likely to improve the chances of quality conference communication including *quality membership*, *goal orientation*, *setting an agenda*, *leadership*, *cooperation versus competition*, and *listening*. Along with this presentation is a discussion of the problems with each of the facilitating components.

QUALITY MEMBERSHIP

Conference communication success depends to a great extent on the population of the group doing the communicating. (If the meeting simply is a presentation of information by a single speaker, then it is essentially a presentation and doesn't fall into the category of meetings—see Chapter 6.)

The primary reason for meeting as a group is the desire for group interaction. Effective communication in group contexts does not mean just meeting the goals of the conference—it means meeting those goals with the input of those present. This may appear to be an academic distinction, but it is not. If the ostensible reason for meeting as a group is the genuine reason, then there is a desire for all those present to participate in the proceedings. If there is no desire for certain individuals to participate in a meeting, then either screen out these members or recognize the charade for what it is. Such charades will inevitably cause problems, despite their questionable short-term values.

To facilitate effective communication in groups then, conference members need to be responsible to their roles as participants in the process. Frequently, groups are burdened with an assortment of unprepared dolts, fledgling megalomaniacs, sycophantic wimps, pretentious pedants, sententious bores, and narcoleptics. It is essential to purge the membership of these unproductive participants in order to realize effective communication.

Without a quality membership, no strategy for effective conference communication can work.

GOAL ORIENTATION

The goals of a conference must be clear, meaningful, and credible. That is, participants must:

- Have a clear understanding of what they need to do
- Understand the reason for doing it
- Believe that the alleged objectives are bona fide

Consider the following example as it relates to believing in alleged objectives.

Jackson, a veteran employee, volunteered to sit on a committee that would meet to discuss proposed calendar changes for an organization. The RPG organization wanted to restructure its vacation times and deadline schedules to better meet the needs of the growing organization. Jackson was glad to volunteer for this job, because he had long felt that the calendar needed improvement and wanted to participate in such restructuring. Not only did Jackson sit on the committee, but because of his interest and concern for the project, he encouraged other middle-level managers to participate in the meetings as well.

The Calendar Committee, as it came to be called, worked mostly in the evening. After work and after dinner, nine dedicated, veteran employees returned to the company to work on a proposal to submit to top management. After eight meetings, the Calendar Committee came up with a document describing the proposed calendar changes. With pride, Jackson personally brought the document to top management and presented the report.

Three months later Jackson and all other employees received a revised calendar for the RPG organization through interoffice mail. Attached to the calendar was a memo explaining that the schedule would take effect starting with the beginning of the new year.

To Jackson's dismay, the new schedule did not reflect in any meaningful way the contributions of the Calendar Committee. It seemed as if either the committee's recommendation was discarded as inappropriate or simply ignored.

Jackson nearly sprinted to the administrative offices and demanded an explanation. He was told that top management felt, in the final analysis, that scheduling was an administrative decision.

As Jackson relayed this story to me over coffee one day, he both verbally and nonverbally expressed his fury at having donated so many hours to what amounted to a charade. His final remark to me was quite clear.

After he drained his last bit of coffee, he looked at me directly eyeball to eyeball and said, "I will never, ever, sit on a committee in this place again."

If a sentiment such as Jackson's pervades an organization, it will be difficult to get high-quality input from high-quality people. A group can communicate effectively if it has a clear understanding of purpose *and* believes the purpose is genuine.

SETTING AGENDAS

An agenda is simply a schedule to follow for a conference. It describes in detail the issues and order of topics that are to be covered. The items on an agenda, if designed intelligently and covered sequentially, provide a step-by-step method for meeting the goals of the conference. Too many groups meet without a formal agenda. It seems fairly obvious that if each participant is aware of the material to be covered, then that participant could prepare appropriately for the meeting. Additionally, a structured agenda will assist in the identification and clarification, if necessary, of the purposes for the meeting.

Committee participants ought to have an opportunity to participate in the creation of the group's agenda. Announcements should be made informing members of an upcoming meeting and inviting their input on items to be included on the agenda.

A big problem with conference communication is the frequent existence of a hidden agenda. This agenda includes objectives for a meeting that are not on the table but which nevertheless constitute the actual meeting goals of one or more of the participants.

Assume that a group is formed to discuss the credentials necessary for a new hire. The purpose of the meeting is to create a list of characteristics and experiences necessary for the successful candidate. However, if Smith and Jones have a dear friend, Davis, who wants this particular job, Smith and Jones may come to the meeting with a hidden agenda. Smith and Jones may try to engineer the discussion so that the committee creates a list of characteristics and experiences that happen to coincide with Davis's.

Frequently, those who are protective of their own turf will come to meetings that are supposedly held to discuss changes for the good of the whole with a hidden agenda to maintain their own turf. The good of the whole comes in second. Obviously, such hidden agendas can militate against effective conference communication.

LEADERSHIP

Someone in a group setting has to assume certain leadership responsibilities. Even in those groups in which a leader is not officially named, a de facto leader will commonly emerge from the committee population. Leaders in groups have a number of specific responsibilities, including:

- *Get the meeting started.* Group participants often assemble slowly, and preliminary chit-chat sometimes exceeds the appropriate few minutes for such orientation. A leader has the responsibility to make sure that not too much time is wasted at the beginning of a session.

- *Keep the discussion on track.* Conferences are notorious for lengthy digressions. Discussion that might begin with an analysis of departmental purchasing can result in commiserating about the cost of poor Charlie's new fuel pump. A leader has the responsibility to keep the discussion on topic. Conferences typically have time limits and lengthy digressions result in jamming the last few items on the agenda into an inappropriately short time. Some managers deliberately put hot items on the bottom of the agenda list, knowing full well that the group will never get to them, given its propensity for digression. Responsible leaders must be mindful of time and move the meeting accordingly.

- *Summarize periodically.* Because of the different input and the inevitable tangential commenting, it is wise to periodically summarize what has been brought out by various members to clarify where the group is. Such summarizing can often facilitate an appropriate transition to the next topic of discussion.

- *Solicit comments from taciturn members.* Since effective conference communication requires input from all participants, each member must contribute to the proceedings. Often, quiet members need prodding to voice their opinions. "Quiet" is not synonymous with "irresponsible." Taciturn members may be simply quiet and need solicitation and encouragement. Leaders, to the extent that they can, should ensure that reserved participants do contribute to the discussion.

- *Curtail verbose members.* The other side of the problem is the talkative participant. Some people do not realize that they are monopolizing conversation. Others are aware, and have no qualms with such inconsiderate behavior. A leader has the uncomfortable job of intervening when a group member is taking too much time, to allow for other comments and to facilitate progress toward the completion of the meeting's agenda.

- *Reduce interpersonal conflict.* Conflict is endemic to conference communication. As long as there are two sides to an issue, confrontations about the appropriate side are likely. One of the more difficult tasks for a group leader is to diplomatically ride herd over the membership to avoid these inevitable conflicts from affecting the communication process.

- *Conclude the meeting.* Just as the leader has the responsibility to start the meeting, the leader also has the responsibility to end the session. At that time, the leader should summarize the progress of the session, indicate what remains to be done, and announce, if the information is available, when the next meeting will take place.

- *Plan for the next session.* Between meetings, the leader has the job of planning for the next session. This includes sending out the minutes of the preceding session to committee members, taking care of the logistics for the next meeting, such as reserving meeting rooms, making sure the meeting time is appropriate for everyone, and soliciting additional agenda topics for the next session.

Being a leader is not easy. It is a complex task that requires a great deal of diplomacy and communication skill. As American author Caskie Stennett once wrote about diplomats, a leader has to be "a person who can tell you to go to hell in such a way that you actually look forward to the trip." There are many people who have become quite skilled at such conference leadership. Dr. David Hess at the State University of New York at Fredonia was the best that I have ever seen in this capacity. When Hess chaired a meeting, the meeting progressed.

In addition to these skilled leaders, there are also many unskilled leaders. There are those, for example, who volunteer for leadership roles because of the inherent power in the job. This is a potentially disastrous situation. It is difficult enough to diplomatically resolve conflicts in a group, but worse yet by far, if the leader is the source of these conflicts. A loquacious leader can single-handedly reduce a conference to a public speaking presentation.

Similarly, it is surprising to notice the number of conference leaders who are selected by the "not-me" method. There are times when employees volunteer to participate in group projects, but are reluctant to assume the leadership position for any one of a number of reasons.

If no one has been previously assigned leader, one participant will likely ask, "Who wants to assume leadership?" Often the next audible sounds in the conference room consist of a litany of excuses culminating with a series of "not-me's." The last person to say "not me"—the person who was unable to quickly come up with a good enough excuse to preclude the assumption of leadership responsibility—becomes the leader.

Leadership is important for group communication success and care must be taken to ensure that a qualified participant assumes that responsibility.

COOPERATION VERSUS COMPETITION

Obviously, a spirit of cooperation, as opposed to a spirit of competition, facilitates effective communication in groups. This is an item, however, that needs to be placed in the "easier said than done" file. Competition, not cooperation, is the default characteristic of groups.

Consider the next situation. It illustrates the nature of competition in groups, and it occurs each time I conduct a seminar on effective conference communication.

I begin each of these seminars by briefly introducing the program and the purposes of the program. I emphasize that the seminar will deal with improving communication in conferences. I then divide the participants into four groups, and give each group the same problem to solve. After participants read the problem, each group moves to one of the four corners of the seminar room to begin discussion.

The problem the groups are asked to solve involves the ranking of items in terms of each item's importance for society. The list includes religion, education, community health, family, and romantic affiliation. At the end of a certain amount of time, usually thirty minutes, I ask each group to provide a consensus list that ranks these items. In addition, I ask the groups to be able to defend their rankings.

As I observe the individual groups' discussions, I note that the interaction within the groups becomes more heated as time goes on. Initially, some members appear to be indifferent about the appropriate ranking, but near the end of the thirty minutes as the group tries to reach consensus, there is contentious debate and very reluctant compromise.

The next step in this exercise is particularly noteworthy. After each group has presented its consensus ranking, I select one representative from each group and have the four selected representatives form another group that meets in the middle of the seminar room. I request that this new group attempt to come up with a consensus that reflects the sentiments of the entire seminar.

As the discussion begins, it becomes apparent that each representative is not concerned with forming a consensus, but rather wants to "win" the discussion for the home group. The nature of the discussion in the center is furious. Additionally, each representative has a bona fide cheering section shouting encouragement from the various corners of the room.

Don't give in Pamela.
Hang tough, Jim. Hang tough.
You're wimping out, Chuck!

I have heard each of these outbursts (and worse) during this exercise. The primary agenda has succumbed to the hidden agenda of winning—and winning, no less, for a position that most of the participants were not terribly concerned with thirty-five minutes before. In a less dramatic way, this phenomenon is typical of many group encounters, and is the reason why cooperation is rare in group contexts.

What happens in groups is that participants become ego-involved. That is, a discussant's posture on an issue becomes intertwined with that person's ego. Tom's *position* on the new hire becomes *Tom's* position on the new hire. If people attack the position, they attack Tom. Therefore, since this phenomenon is rather common, groups often become competitive. Simply, participants stop wanting to discuss the merits of an issue. They often just want to win.

As the group increases in number and as the screening of membership becomes more relaxed, the competitive characteristic of groups becomes more and more likely. As Alexander Hamilton wrote in *The Federalist*, "The more numerous an assembly may be, of whatever characters composed, the greater is known to be the ascendency of passion over reason."

LISTENING

As mentioned in previous chapters, people are more adept at feigning attention than paying attention. In groups, this phenomenon is as common as in other communication contexts. Listening, of course, is important to group success as only one person can be heard at one time. At that time, the others need to be listening in order to react intelligently. There will be a presentation in this section of two concepts regrading listening. One is related to a general listening pattern, and the other is a framework for improving listening skill. One listening concept is related to a general listening pattern, and another is a framework for improving listening skill.

Differential Time

Ralph Nichols, a researcher on listening, discusses differential time in his writings. As a pioneer scholar in the field of listening, he has written a number of articles on the subject and coauthored the book, *Are You Listening?* His article, "Unto You That Hear," is as clear a piece on the pragmatics of listening as one can find. In this article, Nichols explains the characteristics of poor listeners and recommends methods for improving listening. His primary suggestion is that listeners must understand and use something he refers to as *differential time.*

The essence of differential time is that receivers can listen much more rapidly than speakers can speak since speakers tend to pause periodically, repeat information, and digress. It might take a speaker, for example, sixty seconds to make a point that a listener can consume and understand fully in ten seconds.

In this example, the listener has fifty seconds worth of differential time with which to play. Many listeners waste this differential time by going on cerebral holiday. By the time the listener returns from celestial reverie, the speaker has proceeded to another point. At this point, the listener usually does not scramble to get back on track, but decides "the heck with it" and takes off again for turf unknown. This, obviously, poses a problem for listening.

Active Listening

The solution that Nichols suggests to deal with the reality of differential time is for listeners to be active while listening. To put it in terms of baseball, an infielder prepares for the batted ball by getting in position to move to where the ball might be hit. When the batter connects, the infielder moves to the ball to meet it in order to receive it cleanly.

Most listeners, unlike infielders, do not move a muscle to facilitate receipt of messages, let alone "get in position" before the "pitch" is thrown. The attitude of most listeners is, "If the ball connects with my glove, then fine, otherwise let the outfielders pick it up, I'll get it eventually."

Obviously the tendency to do this depends on the importance of the information to the "infielder." Often, retrieving the valuable information from the "outfielder" is not too difficult, so most "infielders" do not go out of their way for the ball.

A good listener has to be active and ready to pounce on information. During differential time periods, an effective listener stays active by recapitulating what has been previously said and anticipating the next point, all the while staying ready for anything novel.

Active listening is difficult, primarily because it is exhausting for those who have not previously exercised the "muscles" necessary for effective listening. For those who want to become effective participants in groups, however, active listening is an effective way to improve listening skills. And for groups to be successful, the participants within the groups must be active listeners.

STRUCTURING PROCEDURE

Assuming all other factors have been dealt with, the step-by-step application of a structural format can help groups meet their conference goals.

Step 1: State the problem in terms of a series of questions.

After clearly identifying the problems and issues at hand, the group should write these problems/issues as a series of questions that need to be answered. For example, a meeting to discuss hiring for the new vice president position, might result in questions like:

- Do we really need a new vice president?
- What experience do we want the successful candidate to have?
- What salary are we willing to offer such a person?
- What (new) responsibilities will this person have?
- Do we need/want to have an external search?

In order for this step-by-step process to work, these questions have to be identified and enumerated so that all participants are, without exception, aware of each question to be addressed. In addition, the questions must be comprehensive to the extent that the responsible answering of all questions will yield a complete response to the committee's overall goals.

Step 2: Analyze each of the questions.

In this stage, discussants operationally define any key terms that are found in any of the subquestions, and determinations are made regarding what type of information will be required in order to answer each question. For the third question above, for example, there might need to be some research done to discover what money is available and what the national salary range typically is for people of this management level.

Again, as was the case in the first stage, all information that needs to be researched must be specified and listed so that there can be no doubt as to precisely what the committee needs to do.

Step 3: Research the questions.

Whatever investigation needs to be done takes place during this stage. Typically, participants will be assigned "homework" to be completed before the next meeting. There are two schools of thought regarding researching problems in group contexts. One is to assign all discussants to research all issues germane to the problem at hand. The other suggests that the research work should be divided in order to avoid duplication of efforts.

An advantage to the first position is that in this way all participants will become well-versed in all matters related to the problem. To have intelligent discussion, everyone must be intelligently informed. If material is divided up, certain people become expert in their particular areas, but there is no real ability to debate the issues knowledgeably because only a few have the requisite knowledge. The second advantage to this approach is that it is a safeguard against irresponsibility or legitimate excuses for not dealing with an assigned topic. If Robin has to go to Milwaukee to deal with a family matter, the committee can still function. If Robert is one of the lazy dolts referred to in a previous section, the committee can still function.

The advantage to the second school of thought is that it allows for a more in-depth analysis of each specific problem assigned. Also, as mentioned, there is less likelihood of overlap.

The second method is likely to be better than the first only in situations in which the membership is very strong. Even so, the first method may be better. Strong members will research all areas in adequate detail, and instead of overlap, there is a likelihood of complementary information surfacing.

Step 4: Present the research to the committee.

At this point each person presents information germane to the questions at hand. There generally should not be discussion on individual points at this time. Each person should have the opportunity to report, without interruption, the research found on the various subjects. It is appropriate for each presenter to clarify issues related to the report when necessary, but debate of the merits of controversial information should wait until the next stage. This uninterrupted reporting aids the process by avoiding time-consuming debate that might be clarified or eliminated by subsequent reports.

Step 5: Evaluate the information.

In this stage the discussants evaluate the merit of all information while staying focused on the questions the group is addressing. The goal at this stage is to define, in the literal sense, responses to the questions that were posed in the initial stage of this procedure.

Step 6: Answer the questions.

On the basis of the previous stage's work, the discussants should formulate the responses to the initially posed questions. At this point the discussants must check to make sure that their answers to the questions provide the necessary information to meet the original conference goal. If the group initially asked the wrong questions, it should become uncomfortably apparent at this stage of the game. For this reason, the first and second stages of this approach are the keys to the success of the group, given that all other group communication factors are positive.

Step 7: Put the group's efforts into effect.

If the group was supposed to submit a report on the basis of these discussions, then in this stage that report should be issued to whomever is to receive the material. If a presentation to another body is to be made, the group should decide on what form that presentation should take, prepare the presentation, and deliver it.

This step-by-step method is effective, but it will not preclude the problems referred to in the other parts of this chapter. Given other positive factors, however, it will help solve group communication problems.

SUMMARY

As is apparent from the material presented in this chapter, it is not surprising that group communication is a frustrating enterprise which often results in effective, exasperating interactions. The dynamics of the group process are such that it is almost inevitable that tensions will surface from group contacts.

Nevertheless, meetings are likely to continue to be used as a method of message diffusion, and in many cases meetings ought to be used as a source of message diffusion.

To facilitate success in these communication contexts, conference managers should:

- Make sure that the conference approach is appropriate for the message diffusion need
- Populate groups with efficient members
- Clarify group objectives and make certain that such purposes for meeting are not spurious
- Create agendas for each meeting
- Provide adequate leadership for conferences
- Attempt to foster a spirit of cooperation as opposed to competition (The best way to do this is by populating the group with responsible people.)
- Promote effective listening strategies
- Follow a structured procedure for conference communication

The bottom line, however, is simple. Groups must be comprised of committed, responsible, and intelligent employees. If this is not the case, one can predict with certainty that the group will be "a cul de sac to which ideas are lured and quietly strangled."

9

Conclusion

On his 1964 album, *That Was the Year that Was*, folksinger/satirist Tom Lehrer said,

> One problem that recurs more and more frequently these days in books and plays and movies is the inability of people to communicate with the people they love—husbands and wives who can't communicate, children who can't communicate with their parents and so on. And the characters in these books and plays—and in real life I may add—spend hours bemoaning the fact that they can't communicate. I feel that if a person can't communicate, the very least he can do is to shut up.

Humorist Kin Hubbard offered similar sentiments when he remarked, "Why can't the fellow who says 'I'm no speechmaker' let it go at that, instead of giving a demonstration."

Unfortunately, many managers cannot follow Lehrer's or Hubbard's advice. All managers may not have to make speeches, but all managers must communicate effectively in order to effectively manage.

The argument in this book has been that communication is a component of management, and that managers cannot just "shut up" and become quality managers. In fact, even if managers did just "shut up," they would still be communicating. One cannot *not communicate*.

It has been pointed out that communication is not a frill but an aspect of management that can damage the bottom line. The following narrative dramatically illustrates the nature of managerial problems that can result from inadequate attention to communication-related matters.

> I worked for a reputable catering service. The corporation's top management consisted of only two people. The owner was the president and the owner's nephew was the vice president. I was hired by them to be the personnel manager for their new café that would be housed in an art museum. This was a brand new venture for the corporation, because until this time they only catered private parties.
>
> No one in management—top management or catering managers—had any previous experience in the daily operation of a full-service restaurant. In addition to the problem of basic inexperience, the corporation also had problems with inadequate communication channels. This in turn led to problems with relationships within the corporation. There were no formal channels set up for communication. Any attempt at internal interaction was a "hit-or-miss" situation. I was responsible for the operation of the café, but any decision or employee problem had to be approved by either the owner or his nephew. This task was virtually impossible because neither of these decision-makers were at the restaurant nor could they easily be reached.
>
> Because the upper management was so hard to contact, many of the situations got swept under the rug until they became serious problems. The lack of communication put a strain on all of the relationships within the corporation. I became extremely frustrated with the president and vice president. My employees became equally frustrated with me. While I was responsible for the café's daily operation, I could not make any decision without approval.
>
> This situation continued to deteriorate until it began to affect customer satisfaction and the corporation's profit margin. Because the employees were dissatisfied with their employment situation, they passed their feelings on to the customers. Eventually business began to fall off, and the restaurant became run down before its time.
>
> Finally, the two top people took notice, but it was already too late. The restaurant had lost too much money and too many employees to survive. The management chalked it up to experience, and decided to stick to catering only private parties. I think this was a very bad decision on their part because with proper management this venture could have been extremely lucrative for the corporation.

In order to avoid scenarios like this, organizations need to take proactive steps to decrease the chances of communication breakdown.

Reactive approaches are useful when managers need to react, but proactive approaches can eliminate the need for extensive "reactions."

Management must recognize what types of messages employees need and consider intelligent ways to relay those messages. Organizations need to cultivate and implement viable channels for the transfer of information. Managers need to develop their speaking, writing, and listening skills to fulfill their obligations in presentation, conference, and interpersonal contexts. And perhaps most importantly, managers must create an environment where employees want to work and see work as fulfilling activity. Without that foundation it is likely that the most eloquent managers will be rendered ineffective communicators.

Simply, there needs to be a recognition of the components of managerial communication, and a program that addresses potential communication issues before problems surface. In order to manage effectively, managers must add a new dimension to their managerial repertoire. That dimension is the new key of effective communication.

*   *   *   *

It was said of Abraham Lincoln that his "greatest asset was his ability to express his convictions so clearly and with such force that millions of his countrymen made them their own."

Tacitus, the Greek orator, is alleged to have commented, "The breastplate and the sword are not a stronger defense on the battlefield than eloquence is to a man amid the perils of prosecution."

English playwright Ben Jonson commented, "Talking and eloquence are not the same: to speak and speak well are two things. A fool may talk, but a wise man speaks."

As it relates to organizations, management consultant Peter Drucker said it best when he remarked, "In the very large organization, this ability to express oneself is the most important of all the skills a person can possess."

I suggest that readers conclude this book by attempting to "solve" the problems posed by the cases found in Appendix D. For each case, do two things. One, attempt to suggest a remedy for the problems that exist (reactive solutions to the problem). Two, suggest methods that could have been employed to preempt the problem that surfaced (proactive solutions to the problem).

Appendix A

Annotated Bibliography of Related Books

Berne, E. 1972. *What Do I Say After I Say Hello*. New York: Grove Press.

    Eric Berne is the "father" of transactional analysis. He has written a number of books on the subject, some more esoteric than others. This book is a clear description of communication and "scripting" (referred to in Chapter 7). *What Do I Say* is a good book for those who want to examine the roots of their own communications.

DeVito, J. 1991. *Human Communication*. New York: Harper Collins.

    Joe DeVito is one of the more prolific authors in the field of communication. This book deals with a broad range of subjects relating to human interaction. It is used as a textbook at colleges, but is relatively easy to read as texts go and very comprehensive.

DeVito, J. 1990. *The Elements of Public Speaking*. New York: Harper Collins.

    This book by DeVito focuses specifically on public speaking. There are a number of good speaking books out. Stephen Lucas has published one with Random House, and James McCroskey has one with Prentice-Hall. Any of these three would be valuable as a resource for those who want to improve their public speaking.

Goldhaber, G. 1993. *Organizational Communication.* Dubuque: William C. Brown and Benchmark Publishers.

This is a text for graduate students and upper-level undergraduates in organizational communication. Complete, theoretical, and a good resource for those researching the area. Gary Kreps has written a similar book also called *Organizational Communication.* Both books are good as resources, particularly for those who want to examine the area in depth and review citations of academic journal articles on various organizational communication issues.

James, M. and D. Jongeward. 1971. *Born to Win.* Reading, MA: Addison Wesley.

An easy-to-read explanation of transactional analysis. If readers are interested in exploring TA, I suggest either *Born to Win* or *I'm Okay, You're Okay,* written by Thomas Harris.

Nichols, R. and L. Stephens. 1957. *Are You Listening?* New York: McGraw Hill.

As the title implies, this book deals with the issues of listening. Despite the publication date, it is a valuable resource for those interested in this area.

Terkel, S. 1974. *Working.* New York: Pantheon Press.

I include this book here because *Working* includes a description of various problems faced by employees as perceived/expressed by the employees themselves. The descriptions of work and concerns about work often center around managerial communication issues.

Townsend, R. 1970. *Up the Organization.* New York: Knopf.

A popular and poignant book that may be as refreshing to read in the 1990s as it was in the 1970s.

Appendix B

Resources in Managerial Communication

ORGANIZATIONS

Communispond

Communispond is a consulting organization that conducts various seminars for employees on communication-related issues. 617-241-5800

Information Mapping Incorporated

Located in Waltham, Massachusetts. Information Mapping has created a unique method that can be used for documentation or any other internally published company literature. The IMI method has made many converts. The company will either coach organizations on how to do their own documentation using IMI methodology or will actually write up the documentation for client organizations. 617-890-7003

International Association of Business Communicators

Excellent organization headquartered in San Francisco. The organization attempts to meet the needs of all those who are engaged in business communication activities. IABC administers the Accredited Business Communicator examinations and designations. 1-800-PRO-IABC

Joe Williams Communication

Multifaceted organizational communication consulting company located in Bartlesville, Oklahoma. 918-336-2267

Synectics

Synectics is a Cambridge, Massachusetts, based organization that specializes in creative approaches to group interaction. 617-868-6530

Toastmasters International

Toastmasters is an organization dedicated to improving individuals' speaking skills. It functions as a type of support group for those who seek to improve their communication skills. Members meet regularly and cost is nominal. 714-858-8255

TPC: The Publication Company

TPC: The Publication Company is an organization that will write and produce your internal publications for you. They are located in Detroit, Michigan. 313-963-8500

Zaremba and Associates

It is difficult to be dispassionate when commenting about one's own services. That aside, Zaremba and Associates analyzes group and organizational communication problems and makes recommendations for improvement. In addition, seminars on managerial communication problems and speaking workshops are conducted. 617-894-6982

JOURNALS

Communication World

Communication World is written for and by communication professionals. Very straightforward and easy to read. Reading the publication regularly would give one a clear sense of contemporary issues in managerial communication. Published by International Association of Business Communicators.

Journal of Business Communication

This journal contains academic articles germane to all aspects of business communication. Published by International Association for Business Communication (a different organization than the IABC referred to previously).

Management Communication Quarterly

Similar to the *Journal of Business Communication. MCQ* is devoted to research and opinion on subjects related to management and communication. Both this publication and *JBC* are recommended for those who want to examine current research on the subject of managerial communication.

Vital Speeches of the Day

Vital Speeches is issued twice a month and contains the text of recent speeches delivered by business and political leaders.

OTHER RELATED PUBLICATIONS

There are several academic (i.e., research-related) journals not devoted solely to managerial communication, but likely to have contain articles germane to organizational communication issues. These include:

- *Communication Monographs*—published by Speech Communication Association.
- *Communication Quarterly*—published by Eastern Communication Association.
- *Human Communication Research*—published by International Communication Association.
- *The Journal of Applied Communication Research*—published by Speech Communication Association.
- *Journal of Communication*—published by International Communication Association.
- *The Quarterly Journal of Speech*—published by Speech Communication Association.

Appendix C

Related Writings

The following three articles are pieces that are, to my way of thinking, very relevant to the subject of managerial communication.

The first article describes the importance of interpersonal sensitivity for effective organizational interaction. The second discusses the relationship of new technology to managerial communication. The third article is based on the concept of receiver orientation and its significance in managing information.

* * * *

TURN THE BEAT AROUND:
MEETING HUMAN COMMUNICATION NEEDS

"Mr. Seviroli, how was the percussion?"

The issues surrounding this question uttered thirty years ago are at the heart of quality communication in organizations. The inquiry was made in 1962 by Stephen Hill, a sixth-grade ne'er do well who banged the drums (indiscriminately it sometimes seemed to me) directly behind my seat as second trumpeter for Mr. Joseph Seviroli's Fern Place Elementary School "band."

137

I was reminded of Hill's query when recently a colleague told me about a local organization that was going to test the quality of their internal communication. When I asked how they would undertake this task, my friend said that the company intended to collect all their "communications" and examine the effectiveness of each. This meant that the organization would examine their newspapers, bulletin boards, e-mail systems, etc. and then draw a conclusion about their overall communication quality.

This company's test results will not be valid. They may discover some valuable information, but they will not find out about essential dimensions of their organization's communication.

Communication Quality and Human Needs

A key element in quality organizational communication relates to managerial sensitivity and effective superior-subordinate interaction. This comment may seem as if it's the stuff of ethereal seventies philosophy, but there is nothing impractical about it. If you want to assess your organization's communication quality, you'll need to examine the quality of the humans who communicate in the organization. Moreover, you'll need to assess your managers' willingness (and ability) to meet the human needs of their subordinates—particularly when communications regarding these needs require perspicacity and diplomacy.

These communications are every bit as important to the overall communication quality of the organization as video tapes, house organs, and e-mail capabilities. In fact, they may be more significant. Interpersonal interaction that is gratuitously brusque, condescending, or otherwise insensitive can affect the entire climate of an organization—indirectly, if not directly, undermining organizational communication and overall quality. And this brings me to Joseph Seviroli's Fern Place Band, Stephen Hill, and Mr. Hill's inquiry.

Controlled Authority

Joseph Seviroli was the leader of the Fern Place band and the instrument teacher for the elementary school. He taught grade school children how to play and then conducted the collective musicians. Seviroli was a kind and patient man. I clearly remember my first trumpet lesson with him. On that day, Seviroli sat with me and two other fledgling trumpeters in the tiny "lesson room"—a space that certainly had been a storage closet at some time in the past. The goal of this initial session was simply to get us to produce a sound from the end of the horn.

The others quickly blurted out something, were dismissed, and told to return to the regular classroom. However, nothing came out of my trumpet. I couldn't get it. I was blowing ferociously trying to make a peep and Seviroli kept sitting there telling me not to panic. Suddenly I connected with a cacophonous blast that nearly rocketed the poor man into the wall. Without so much as a blinking of an eye he told me that I'd done very well and I marched back to my classroom feeling like I'd accomplished something, and eventually I became a member of the band.

Seviroli was no mollusk. For some reason the entire band, particularly the percussion section, seemed to be populated by wise guys, classmates who, like the aforementioned Hill, when not banging the drums might otherwise be unleashing their energy in societally counterproductive ways. Yet Seviroli kept us in check. He seemed to have the right combination of control and support. We had become, the percussionists and others, truly a band of young kids following the lead of our respected director. The payoffs were internal, more than anything else.

For weeks, if not months, the band was preparing for the big musical spectacular that annually was the event of events for the school. We were to accompany the Fern Place thespians in some original musical. While Seviroli led the band, a Mr. Mushnick directed the stage actors. Mushnick was no Seviroli. He may have been as musically talented, but the man was a screamer. Unlike Seviroli, Mushnick could lose control easily and go into tirades that were remarkable and, apparently, memorable. While bellowing admonishments, his face would contort as if he were holding in his breath for some contest. After he began one such outburst, Stephen Hill leaned over to me and whispered, "Hey, watch this one now. Watch the veins pop out of his head."

So it was Seviroli and Mushnick leading our troops with different styles. Seviroli with strong controlled authority led the band below and Mushnick, without the same control—but with more volume—led the actors above us.

Got to Have Percussion

Nerves became severely frayed as the day of the event approached. Each rehearsal had one form of crisis or another and Mushnick, under what must have been considerable pressure real or imagined, was spewing volcanically at least once an hour. One particular scene in the show had become a recurring problem. In it, a group of child actors emerged from audience level while singing to our music. They were to access the stage by climbing a short set of stairs that were near the percussion section of the band. We musicians were supposed to keep playing until the actors were all in place at their spots on the stage. Almost every time we rehearsed this scene something would go wrong. The actors wouldn't find their spots; the band would stop playing too soon; some of the kids would stop singing while they climbed the stairs— something would go wrong.

The day before opening night, during dress rehearsal, this scene from the Styx took a dive for the worse. It became clear that with costumes and various props the actors would have a difficult time negotiating the walk around the percussion section to gain access to the stage. Mushnick became absolutely enraged by what must have seemed like a conspiracy and burst into a panicked screeching during which he shouted that there were too many drummers and that we simply couldn't have that many. From his perch on the stage he pointed down to Hill who was the last drummer in the line and told him that he had to go.

This, to me, was unthinkable. I couldn't imagine how I would have felt if after all this time I would be booted from the band. I turned around and saw that most of the members were stunned. Big, tough Stephen Hill was crying eleven-year-old tears. Seviroli waved to Hill as if to say not to worry. He hoisted himself on the stage and put his arm around Mushnick. Within minutes the matter seemed to be resolved. Seviroli moved the drums around a bit, and Stephen Hill could stay.

We went through the scene, and it worked just fine. We belted out the music, and the thespians accessed the stage. And then, during the temporary break that followed, Stephen Hill, this truculent young tough, who went on to a career of petty theft and various scrapes with the law, asked both plaintively and genuinely,

"Mr. Seviroli. How was the percussion?"

Seviroli made the okay sign. I turned around and saw Hill positively beaming.

If an organization wants to test the effectiveness of its internal communication, it needs to begin by looking at personnel. They, more than the internal newsletter, will determine the communication efficiency and quality.

We all need to do something meaningful in the band we call our work. And we need to have that work meaningfully acknowledged. As Vickie Sue Robbins crooned, "Turn the beat around."

"Got to Have Percussion."

*   *   *   *

TECHNOLOGY AND QUALITY COMMUNICATION

Introduction

A short while ago I was reading a paper on the 1984 Meese Commission on Pornography. In 1984, as you may recall, President Reagan had appointed the then-Attorney General Edwin Meese to head a group that would assess the impact of pornography on behavior. The assumption was that viewing pornographic materials had an effect on the viewers' tendencies to act out in societally unacceptable manners.

As it turned out, the commission's findings were inconsistent with their hypotheses. That is, viewing societally unacceptable behavior appeared, on the basis of the research, to have no significant effect on consumers' tendencies to engage in similarly unacceptable behavior. Since the findings were wholly inconsistent with the committee's predictions of what they were likely to find, the committee essentially argued that the research must have been flawed.

As it relates to this article, the significance of this paper is not the findings of the Meese Commission nor the Commission's reaction to the results. What is significant is that while reading the paper I noticed two remarkable errors in the text. These errors were the result of inattentive use of a relatively new communication technology.

The point of this article is related to technology. Specifically, it is important for quality communicators to remember that the "bottom line" of efficient communication is the accurate receipt of information. New technologies in and of themselves may be impressive, but do not necessarily eliminate the need to remain focused on the objective of careful transfer of information.

Regain; Mess

The article on the Pornography Commission argued that President Reagan had appointed the Commission in part to placate both conservative groups and feminist groups who were concerned with the rampant spread of pornography. The author of the article commented that the president had been particularly concerned with the feelings of these two groups because of the upcoming election which he wanted, of course, to win.

In this serious piece, each time the author referred to the president, the president's name was written "Regain." It was President "Regain," then, who commissioned the then-attorney general to head this committee. It was President "Regain" who wanted to win reelection. Instead of Edwin Meese, the head of the committee was called, incredibly, Attorney General "Equine Mess."

At first reading, I was so taken by both errors that I was truly nonplused. Then I wondered if the author hadn't cleverly played with the names for some punning value. "Regain" might fit with the President's alleged desire to curry favor with the conservative and feminist groups for purposes of furthering his reelection chances. The author of the article was clear about the inappropriateness of the Meese Commission to reject the research findings because they were inconsistent with the original hypotheses, so, perhaps, "Equine Mess" was some crude pun. However, as I reflected on it for some time, I knew that this was no clever punster. The paper was a serious academic one, and regardless of the disapproval of a commission head, one is unlikely to be so coarse as to refer to the attorney general of the United States so pejoratively.

It was apparent, then, that what had happened was that the author had run a spell check on his piece and had been sloppy with it. Those of us who read and edit internal and external organizational communications will often see this firsthand when we notice the proliferation of words spelled incorrectly because they are homonyms; e.g., " 'There' going to need some help over in marketing" and " 'Are' line of clothes include garments that the 'hole' family can 'where'."

Technology and Communication Quality

I have stressed in the previous paragraphs the fundamental concept of "receiver orientation." This means that a message has not been communicated unless a message has been received. Technological advances are valuable for communicators if they indeed can facilitate the accurate receipt of information.

Certainly, spell check and word processing software in general are absolutely godsends for those in the communication business. The ability to write, rewrite, cut, paste, and edit is so phenomenal that those of us who wrote extensively before the advent of word processing now wonder how we did it. I can recall when Co-Rec type came on the market and I marvelled at this innovation. Now Co-Rec type is a bona fide relic. When the IBM Selectric typewriters came out which actually had Co-Rec type in them, we thought that the invention of all time had surfaced. Now, few who write extensively would choose to use a typewriter when they could work on a computer with word processing software. It is, in short, great for communicators.

However, its capacity for greatness does not guarantee greatness. The wonders of spell check do not obviate communicators' responsibilities.

E-Mail, et al

Similarly other miracles of the twentieth century have the capacity to streamline the communication process. However, they don't necessarily guarantee quality communication. Consider electronic mail. In moments I can send messages to colleagues throughout the world. I can send the same message to many instantaneously. It is a remarkable communication tool.

Yet e-mail is not a panacea for problems with communication quality. It is particularly not a panacea if an organization assumes that because of electronic mail there *should* be few communication problems within the organization.

E-mail may be rapid, but it doesn't guarantee receipt. Some researchers claim that well over 50 percent of what we perceive as meaningful when communicating is derived from nonverbal components of the message being sent. With e-mail there are few nonverbal components to the message. One of the marvels of e-mail is the capacity for instantaneous feedback; however, this capacity doesn't guarantee the feedback in the same way that phone conversations or any face-to-face interaction might. The point is that quality communicators can't assume that the e-mail innovation should replace other forms of internal organizational communication. Certainly e-mail does not obviate concern for communication quality.

Our phone systems in the nineties are typically sophisticated in terms of capabilities. We can conference call, call forward, hold many calls simultaneously, etc. Yet managers concerned with communication quality must acknowledge that the phones' capacities do not guarantee their usage consistent with these capacities. Transferring a call with most systems is the simplest of basic tasks. Yet it's surprising how many persons—particularly in higher-level positions—cannot perform this simple task. I am amused when I hear colleagues tell me that they'll "try" to forward me to another, as if they need to steel themselves for the challenge. One Boston area chief executive refuses to use his voice-mail system because of basic technophobia. If a phone system has conference call potential, but if employees don't utilize it correctly, then the technology hasn't advanced communication quality.

Summary

Advances in technology do not necessarily guarantee communication quality. Communications and communicators can be inefficient regardless of how efficient and/or attractive a communication innovation may be. Without human attention to detail and quality, the product may be something akin to "equine mess."

*   *   *   *

MANAGING INFORMATION

For six weeks during the winter of 1992 I routinely collected every written piece of internal correspondence I received at work. Whenever a memo, brochure, notice, or announcement came to me from any source within my organization, I placed the missive in a cardboard box.

I received more than one hundred such printed messages (the total of one hundred does not include any e-mail, voice mail, or telephone messages). They originated from many different sources, and the message content varied greatly.

There were notices about new organizational policy and reminders of old policy; announcements about upcoming events; minutes from various committees and internal governing bodies; booklets regarding news in other organizational units; notices about food service; and social news on activities that would take place outside of the workplace.

Most, nearly all, of these printed communications I collected were intelligently organized, efficiently written, and attractively printed. Most, if not all, of the sources for these messages believe that they have communicated their messages. They haven't. All they did was distribute information.

Communication, by definition, requires receipt. Dissemination of information is a step in the process, but it is not the sole component of the process. If we assume that effective internal communication affects organizational quality, but we function as if distribution of information defines communication, it is inevitable that communication, and consequently, organizational quality will suffer. Accurate messages may not be read. Memoranda from sources with suspect credibility may be viewed with skepticism. Unclear directives may not compel receivers to contact the source for clarification. Inaccurate information may be acted on as if it were correct. Obviously, production quality can suffer.

Of the documents I collected, some—very few—were inherently flawed. For example, some announced events that had already taken place. There were those that contained inaccuracies that were confusing. One announced a deadline of Thursday the 14th, when Thursday was actually the 16th. In addition, I received several documents which asked me to disregard previously received ones or to make a correction on an earlier notice. Of course, the sender assumes in these instances that the receiver will get the correction, read the correction, and be familiar enough with the earlier correspondence to see the relevance of the new one.

Even when the correspondence was impeccable—accurate, timely, clear, credible, and well written—the presumption of communication was inaccurate. Some receivers simply don't read well or are put off when they see lengthy documents.

Some employees are so swamped with printed information that they couldn't read everything they get without reneging on their other organizational responsibilities. Employees are not necessarily delinquent ne'er do wells if they haven't thoroughly read all correspondence.

It is interesting to note that I received a number of messages that were sent to me when they should have been directed to someone else. The forwarding of such misdirected information may be only a minor nuisance. Yet this type of error can result in more serious problems that insidiously affect organizational quality. Consider the following.

A colleague received an envelope addressed to him that had been stamped CONFIDENTIAL in red on several places on the envelope. It had been sent via inter-office mail. He opened the CONFIDENTIAL correspondence and read the letter enclosed.

He was delighted to read that he had been awarded a salary increase. This was fantastic news. It was a significant sum and, moreover, the apparent raise had come during an "increment freeze" in the organization. Therefore, the awarding of this additional money was not only welcome, but also an apparent reflection of management's recognition of excellent performance.

After the initial moment of elation, my colleague reread the letter and was stunned when he noticed that the letter, in fact, was not addressed to him, but to one of his coworkers.

The author of the correspondence thought my colleague was the awardee's supervisor and had "copied" him with the news of the increment. Years before my colleague had been an interim supervisor, but now was the awardee's peer, a coworker. Obviously, the author/source had copied the wrong person and fueled some interesting speculation. "How come Charlie got a raise during the 'increment freeze'?" One can imagine how this gaffe affected interpersonal harmony within the department. Communication disasters of this type are certainly the exception rather than the rule, but the consequences may be dramatic nevertheless.

Two fundamental steps toward managing information are (1) recognizing the impact communication can have on organizational quality, and consequently, considering it a "front-burner" issue and (2) adopting a receiver-oriented perspective with your communication. That is, assume that "message communicated" is defined as, message received, consumed, and understood.

Information, Networks, and Relationships

Beyond recognition and this receiver orientation, to be proactive in terms of communication, organizations need to address three essential aspects of internal communication. They are (1) the nature and types of information that need to be sent to members of the organization, (2) the avenues that are available for the distribution of this information, and (3) the relationships of organizational members that can facilitate or retard the communication of information.

A quality organization needs to identify what kinds of information employees need in order to function effectively. Nearly every business needs to clearly articulate policies, job expectations of employees, and performance appraisal. Management must intelligently examine how well this information is being communicated to employees. Is the information being distributed? Is it being distributed using a method that is likely to assure accurate receipt?

A quality organization needs to create channels that allow messages to move from one person to another. For example, there needs to be meaningful subordinate-to-superior networks. If a superior, as a rule, discourages subordinate contact, then the channel that could permit valuable information to travel from subordinate to superior is spurious at best. Superiors may never discover that there are problems on lower levels. They may miss out on some good ideas from subordinates. They may assume that all messages sent to subordinates from superiors were received with understanding and agreement. And they may discover that the absence of a subordinate-to-superior network can erode morale.

A quality organization needs to recognize that the "climate" of an organization has a discernible impact on communication. Interpersonal relationships can encourage or discourage employees from exercising their speaking, writing, and listening skills. The ability to write and speak well can be relatively insignificant if employee relationships have been aggravated. Information may be slow to move from department to department if unresolved conflict exists.

In short, communication affects quality. Quality managers examine what needs to be communicated, how it should be communicated, and how one can create an environment that is conducive to effective communication.

Appendix D

Cases for Analysis

The three cases below can be used for group diagnosis and discussion. How would you deal with the issues presented in the cases and how would you address the requests made of you as indicated in each case?

CASE ONE—DAVIS PAPER

An organization that manufactures stationery and stationery products operates two facilities for the creation and distribution of their products. Both plants house approximately 250 employees each. The facilities need to interact in order to function and presently rely on phones and a courier system to link the locations. There is a fax machine located in the suburban offices, but it is used almost solely for external contacts, i.e., to communicate with customers.

The original facility was built in Boston. When the organization needed more space and wanted to expand, the business built the second facility. This facility was, of course, more modern than the first building. It was constructed in Carlisle, a relatively rural suburb. The newer building had ample parking space, handsome offices, bucolic surroundings for lunchtime walks or jogging, and in general, a sweeter atmosphere than the facility in town. Shortly after the construction of the second building, many of the executives of the company moved out to the suburban facility.

After a number of years, the people at the newer plant began to get a reputation as snobs whereas those at the city plant began to be referred to disparagingly as slobs. Old-timers who worked at the downtown location referred to Carlisle workers as "yuppie scum."

An executive for the organization, sensing a morale problem, suggested a cocktail hour type get-together for the suburban and urban employees. The plan was approved and a memo was written to announce the cocktail reception and urge attendance. The memo read:

> As we all are aware, there is some dissension here at Davis Paper. For reasons that are difficult to determine, there is a bit of a rift which exists between the suburban employees and our brethren working in the city. This lack of unity is bad for Davis, and we are doing something to try to remedy and rectify this situation.
>
> This Friday we will be throwing a cocktail "hour" from six to eight at the Executive Room at the Marriott in Auburndale. Please join us there for cocktails, a light dinner, and the camaraderie which will make Davis a better place to be. Remember our slogan, "It's Write with Davis!"

Because of a delivery snafu, the message did not get to the employees at the downtown facility until the Monday after the scheduled reception. The employees at the suburban plant attended with a few of the urban employees who had gotten the message through the grapevine. The conversations at the party consisted mostly of pejorative jokes directed at the inner-city "slobs." As a result of this snafu, the situation at the plants continued to deteriorate.

You have been contacted by the director of personnel for Davis Paper. Her office is at the Carlisle location (as is the case with all vice presidents and directors except the director of maintenance and organizational sanitation). She asks you to make recommendations regarding the problems at Davis. She tells you that you will be competing with other consulting companies for a long-term contract to work with Davis Paper.

Specifically, the director of personnel asks for:

- A short-term (reactive) solution to the memo snafu.
- A long-term (proactive) plan for good communication.
- Suggestions for an external communication plan to restore what Davis senses is a deteriorating image.
- A written proposal as well as an oral presentation which articulates your suggestions. In the written proposal, she asks that you supply a budget for your recommended suggestions. For all proposals, the budget is not to exceed $100,000 for any initial expenditures. If any suggestions are annual/ongoing (e.g., a new position), you may allot $30,000 only for any ongoing costs.

CASE TWO—MELLOW BLEND TOBACCO

MELLOW BLEND Inc. produces pipes and pipe accessories. The entire operation is housed in one four-story building. The president and his suite of offices are on the top floor. In addition to the president's own office, there are two auxiliary offices to the president and a conference room. On the door to the president's office hangs a large painting of a pipe. There is also a large poster with the words "MELLOW BLEND Will Not Go Up In Smoke" written on it. This poster looks like it was a gift by employees as there are many signatures on the poster. Ironically, a sign has been placed on all of the desks on the fourth floor including the President's that reads, "Thank You for Not Smoking."

Four vice presidents have offices on the third floor. These vice presidents are the executive vice president, administrative vice president, production vice president, and the special vice president. (This special vice president position was created two years previously to employ the president's nephew.)

There are twelve supervisors who work under the vice presidents. These employees are on the second floor. Each supervisor is responsive to the six divisions of MELLOW BLEND. These divisions are external affairs; pipe production; pipe cleaners and accessories; pipe tobacco; engineering and experimentation; and maintenance and clerical. Essentially two supervisors work with each division. There is no clear delineation of job responsibility between the two supervisors for each division.

On the first floor or ground level are the department heads, senior employees, and junior employees. The department heads are supervisors of units within each division. For example, in the maintenance and clerical division, there are the units of repairs, cleaning (floors and offices), cleaning (equipment), cleaning (lavatories), secretaries (executives), secretaries (supervisors), etc. There are 412 employees who work for MELLOW BLEND. The number of employees is not evenly divided in each division.

Senior employees are those who have twenty years (or more) of loyal service to MELLOW BLEND. One can also become a senior employee prematurely if that individual has given "meritorious" service to the organization. Such designations are made by the administrative vice president after recommendations by the appropriate supervisor. Junior employees get less sick leave, less vacation time, and although not formal policy, more of the menial jobs. Senior employees also get to wear identification tags which read: SENIOR EMPLOYEE, JOHN SMITH.

There is little contact between the plant level and the other levels of the organization.

Identified Problems

The executive vice president of MELLOW BLEND contacts you. He tells you that MELLOW BLEND has conducted an in-house survey to assess the situation. The problems identified in the survey are listed on the next page.

1) All employees feel that senior employees do little work.
2) Junior employees feel angry and belligerent.
3) Engineering and external affairs departments do not communicate well because of a snafu that occurred years ago.
4) Maintenance and clerical division employees feel like second class citizens.
5) Department heads resent supervisors because they feel that the supervisors do little work. Most employees feel that the vice presidents do little else but take long lunch breaks.
6) The president has taken a laissez-faire attitude, having given all CEO responsibilities to the executive vice president but retaining the figurehead position of president. Most employees see the president as an elderly buffoon who can't stand smoke but who owns a tobacco company. There is almost no employee contact with either the president or the executive vice president. The upward networks are not there.
7) The production division has accrued a bevy of incompetents and the organization's name is being tarnished by this group. Unfortunately, the employees in this division have somehow become senior employees and for the most part are related to family members in upper-echelon positions in the organization.
8) The external affairs division is not in touch and does not want to be in touch. They are marketing the products without regard to the changing nature of the company. Most of the external affairs people seem to not care that the product has changed and they are selling another product.
9) No one can figure out what the special vice president is supposed to do. There is resentment regarding the special vice president on every level of the organization (except the president).
10) The rules and regulations bulletin is outdated and includes items like, "No employees may have facial hair." No one pays attention to these ancient items, and therefore, the whole rules and regulations bulletin is a joke.

The executive vice president asks you to do two things. They are:

- Present an oral analysis of the identified problems to a group of MELLOW BLEND executives.
- Prepare a two-page, "reader-friendly" document that describes your solutions to the problems.

Remember that the key to effectiveness with internal communication is to make sure that messages, networks, and relationships within the organization are healthy.

CASE THREE—BATTLESHIPS RESTAURANTS

Introduction

BATTLESHIPS is a continent-wide chain of restaurants that specializes in overstuffed submarine sandwiches. Their motto is, "Why have a SUB when you can have a BATTLESHIP?"

In addition to "Battleships" (the name for the sandwich), entries include very large salads, pizza, pasta dishes, and nearly anything one could find on a menu in an I-Hop or at a diner. In general, Battleships caters to voracious eaters and offers very large portions of nearly everything they list on the menu. Unusually large breakfasts are also served from 7 a.m. to 10 a.m. each day.

The restaurants stay open as late as local municipalities permit. Beer and wine (no other alcohol) is served throughout the day during times when alcohol is permitted to be served in the respective municipalities.

Locations and Organization

These restaurants are located near universities in the following cities:

Orono	Columbia	Berkeley	Cambridge
Back Bay	Denver	Montreal	Minneapolis
Vancouver	Pittsburgh	Philadelphia	Toronto
Mexico City	Washington D.C.	New Orleans	Syracuse
Los Angeles	Boulder	Austin	Durham

BATTLESHIPS Central is located in Philadelphia. The first BATTLE-SHIPS opened near the University of Pennsylvania campus. Since then Philadelphia has been the center for operations. BATTLESHIPS Central is located in three offices above the BATTLESHIPS Philadelphia restaurant.

Communications

The staff at BATTLESHIPS Central publish the newsletter titled, *Sink the Sub*. *Sink the Sub* is mailed every two months to managers of each restaurant. Some managers post the newsletter on bulletin boards. Some managers duplicate the newsletter and give a copy to each employee. Some managers simply leave copies around the restaurant. *Sink the Sub* includes social news sent in by managers who are inclined to send in such information. It also includes upbeat information about what's news in culinary arts. It is a four-page, "non-glossy" publication without color or professional organization.

The restaurants all have phones, but it is rare that any BATTLESHIPS restaurant is contacted by phone by BATTLESHIPS Central. Most correspondence is handled through U.S. mail. The correspondence that does exist includes *Sink the Sub*, statements of earnings for each restaurant in the chain (published quarterly), occasional letters applauding the efforts of all managers, and letters regarding financial matters related to the operation that managers must read and respond to.

There is no company-wide Rules and Regulations Manual and no company-wide training procedure. BATTLESHIPS Central does publish a one-sheet guideline regarding BATTLESHIPS policy. However, it is a vague document and is only sent to new managers, not new employees. Also, there are times when BATTLESHIPS Central does not know about managerial changes. In those cases, of course, the new manager does not even get this vague letter.

Each store has a fax machine, but no specific policy regarding what types of messages should be sent on it. The fax is used as much by customers who fax in their orders as by BATTLESHIPS management. Central uses it primarily when there is some kind of emergency. Each restaurant manager controls a budget that includes discretionary moneys for innovations.

Problem

In December, a letter was written to BATTLESHIPS Central from BATTLESHIPS Back Bay. The letter appears below:

> Representatives of Battleships Central:
>
> I am a waiter at BATTLESHIPS in Boston (the one in Back Bay—not the one in Cambridge). I want you to know that the restaurant operation here is a joke. I have worked here for five weeks, and the manager barely speaks with me.
>
> Besides, I've never formally been trained, and I often do not know what I'm supposed to be doing. The manager used to be a waiter here and seems to be very close with the other waiters, but I hear little from him and receive the worst shifts and the worst stations.
>
> We serve sandwiches, salads, and pizza here, and I want you to know that every day some jerk (who is chummy with the manager) brings in some reeking Chinese food in those ridiculous cardboard boxes and makes an absolute sight of himself pigging out on the Chinese food (and spreading the aroma) right in front of the customers.
>
> It's ridiculous! Do you want to encourage people to go elsewhere? Have you no policies? Do you care if anyone adheres to them? Somehow I think it is inappropriate for workers to be eating Chinese food in BATTLESHIPS. I think the organization is run by fools!
>
> Also, you aren't aware of it, but you are in for big trouble around here if you're not careful. The "jocks" come in at 10 p.m., and have their Battleships. That's fine. But they also start quaffing

the beer. AND MOST OF THESE GUYS ARE UNDERAGE. When it gets out that BATTLESHIPS serves minors, do you know what will happen to the entire chain?

There are many times I want to tell the managers how they could improve the place, but they never want to listen. They essentially tell me to be quiet or respond with their standard refrain, "If it's not broke, don't fix it." Well, you need to know that if "it's not broke" yet, it's on the way to breaking.

Morale is very low here and the integrity of your entire operation is in question. I want you to know that if I don't hear from BATTLESHIPS Central within two weeks, I am positively going to contact *Boston Business Magazine*, the *Wall Street Journal*, and *Fortune* with this letter. I also want you to know that I have a buddy at BATTLESHIPS Mexico City who says that the situation is *worse* there. You idiots send them *Sink the Sub* in English. Unbelievable!

Since I fear retribution if I am identified, I will ask you to contact me by writing to "Mike" at P.O. Box 1239, Boston, MA. Thank you for your attention to this letter.

Mike

The people at BATTLESHIPS Central receive this letter and contact you, a consultant. BATTLESHIPS recognizes that "Mike's" complaints are not off the mark. They have heard similar comments in the past. They ask you to develop a specific communication plan that will deal with the following.

1) **Organizational Messages**

They want you to recommend what messages they need to send to employees; how to send these messages; and how they can avoid communication breakdown. They want these recommendations on managing information for within each restaurant and throughout the chain.

They also want a recommendation about what they should do about Mike's letter.

(Refer to Chapter 2 for information regarding this item.)

2) **Organizational Networks**

They want you to recommend how to improve the internal networks at BATTLESHIPS both within each restaurant *and* throughout the chain. They are interested in all internal networks (i.e., directional, formal, informal).

(Refer to Chapter 3 for information regarding this item.)

3) Organizational Climates

They want you to recommend how to improve the climate at BATTLESHIPS *in a meaningful way.* That is, both within each restaurant and throughout the chain, how can they create a supportive climate that is not spurious.

(Refer to Chapter 4 for information regarding this item.)

Index